Department of Theological Questions
Irish Inter-Church Meeting

FREEDOM, JUSTICE AND RESPONSIBILITY IN IRELAND TODAY

VERITAS

8/4/2000

First published 1997 by
Veritas Publications
7-8 Lower Abbey Street
Dublin 1

Copyright © Irish Inter-Church Meeting 1997

ISBN 1 85390 396 5

British Library Cataloguing
in Publication Data.
A catalogue record for
this book is available
from the British Library.

Cover design by Banahan McManus Ltd, Dublin
Printed in the Republic of Ireland by Betaprint Ltd, Dublin

The Catholic Church in Ireland
The Church of Ireland
The Greek Orthodox Church in Britain and Ireland
The Methodist Church in Ireland
The Presbyterian Church in Ireland
The Non-Subscribing Presbyterian Church
The Moravian Church in Ireland
The Lutheran Church in Ireland
The Religious Society of Friends
The Salvation army

The views expressed in this document do not necessarily represent those of the Irish Inter-Church Meeting or its Member Churches.

The Irish Inter-Church Meeting
Inter-Church Centre
48 Elmwood Avenue
Belfast BT9 6AZ

October 1996

CONTENTS

PART TWO: THE REALITY OF IRELAND TODAY

FOREWORD

It may be helpful to indicate briefly the process which has led to publication of this document. For some considerable time the Department of Theological Questions has been discussing the differing approaches which exist between – and within – our Churches to the question of how moral decisions and judgments are made.

We had begun to organise our thoughts under the heading of 'Freedom, Justice and Responsibility in Ireland Today' when, in late 1994, the Irish Inter-Church Committee asked that we look at these issues more particularly, as they put it, 'in the light of recent events in the peace process'.

The members of the Department divided themselves into two groups which became known, in a kind of shorthand, as the Vision Group and the Reality Group. The former was to approach the issues mainly from the biblical, theological perspective and the latter from a reflection on the actual situation.

Obviously such a division is far from watertight. The Vision Group would not like to think that it was out of touch with reality; nor would the Reality Group wish to be seen as lacking in vision. It was hoped that the two approaches would converge, and to a great extent they did.

Recent events have offered hope and challenge to all the Churches but they have also revealed the fragility of our hopes. This document reflects on the ingredients of true peace, namely, freedom, justice and responsibility. It seeks to reflect on our common commitment to these values and the ways in which they are understood in our common Christian tradition. It reflects also on the ways in which our religious and cultural traditions may lead to different emphases in our understanding of these values and on how we might reach a fuller understanding of one another's approaches.

One of the most important factors leading to growth of understanding is through action in which we address the real situation in Ireland. This involves both action within individual communions and action jointly undertaken by Churches and by individuals to engage together in the fostering of peace, justice and responsibility in Ireland today. The document, therefore, offers some reflections on the challenges offered by the reality of our situation, North and South, and some suggestions about steps which might form part of a response to that challenge.

PART ONE

BIBLICAL AND THEOLOGICAL PERSPECTIVES

INTRODUCTION
THE CHALLENGES WE FACE

Many facets of life in Ireland face us as Churches with varied challenges. The culture of today contains many expressions of the value of justice, responsibility and freedom. Like any cultural phenomenon these expressions contain some elements which are positive, some which are ambiguous and some which are negative.

The Churches may singly or corporately be able to affirm together what is positive, and to evaluate critically but constructively what is ambiguous or negative. Full and detailed agreement on these questions may not always prove possible. Where it is not, differences should be honestly expressed and the reasons for the differences should be understood as clearly as possible.

The cry 'Freedom' going up from many today has in it elements of a most positive character. It is the cry of the sinner for righteousness, the poor for sustenance, the oppressed for justice, women for fair treatment, dignity and equal opportunities, the underprivileged for support and proper provision to meet their needs. There is at the same time a growing demand for participation which rejects attitudes perceived as authoritarian, whether in Church or State. There is a resistance, by no means confined to the young and dispossessed, to any form of constriction by structures, attitudes or moral rules.

This does, however, contain elements that are at best ambiguous. The demand for freedom can become a tendency to oppose or reject any form of authority, and an attitude which sees every structure as oppressive almost by definition. This can lead to the negative outcome of a radical individualism or a *laissez faire* attitude.

A constructive critique requires a balanced approach to the relationship between freedom and authority, between personal autonomy and objective truth. It requires an understanding and an exercise of authority which sees it as the enabling basis and even inspiration of true freedom.

In Ireland today the cultural expression of freedom, justice and responsibility has a particular resonance. People, both North and South, are rightly demanding equality of status, justice and peace – freedom from fear, intimidation, discrimination, violence and the positive hope for a better life. At the same time we face the challenge of ensuring a permanent end to violence and creating a durable political settlement.

The continuing reality of sectarianism poses a particular challenge to the Churches. We must take effective steps to ensure that religious belief is, as it should be, a source of reconciliation and peace, that it fosters freedom, justice and responsibility. When it is seen as being associated with hatred, prejudice and injustice, that is a scandal which has to be addressed.

Where constructive criticism reveals attitudes, whether in Church or State, which are destructive of freedom, justice and responsibility, openness and humility are required in order to recognise and correct what is wrong. This requires an approach which expresses one's own point of view in truth and love and which recognises the freedom of others to do the same, however much one may disagree.

Freedom, justice and responsibility in the **political** arena require respect for the principle of consent between the two communities in Northern Ireland, in the relationship between North and South, and between the United Kingdom and the Republic of Ireland. These intermeshing relationships imply a duty to speak the truth to one another in love, to seek justice for all, not only for one's own group, and to have concern each for the other.

Freedom, justice and responsibility in the **social** arena require a critique of the structures leading to unemployment and inequality and the search for a social order where opportunities are open to all. Other elements of social life which diminish people mentally, physically and spiritually, and which can wreck lives, include drug abuse, pornography and unjust discrimination on grounds such as race, gender or religion. Freedom, in other words, should be freedom *with* and for one another and *from* the things that destroy and divide.

We clearly have a duty to oppose such negative factors. In particular, secular humanism, the rejection of God, cannot be accepted by Christians as right or as creative of human freedom. It is the denial of what the Churches stand for. The absence of God in the secular order of much of our western society has been spoken of as 'the increasingly open wound of the European mind'.[1] This is not to deny that the so-called secular approach has, in many ways, also made a positive contribution. It can, for instance, look at religious division and sectarianism from a perspective which may allow them to be seen in a new light.

The obscuring of the divine – the loss of transcendence, the spirit of apathy, the tendency to treat faith as a private matter divorced from the total context in which it is to be found and lived – is profoundly misleading and misguided.

The concept of love as it is expressed in the New Testament is the highest goal of freedom. We are called to use our freedom by giving ourselves in love to God and to one another. The concept can, however, be misinterpreted in a sentimental sense or seen in purely physical terms as in the phrase 'making love'. In such ways it is divorced from the totality of personal relationships in which love should be expressed in mutual trust, fidelity and commitment. Liberty misinterpreted in these ways can degenerate rapidly into licence.

A growing pluralism poses the question as to how best we can accommodate differences of culture, race and creed with 'no surrender' of principle, while, at the same time, being 'a risen people' capable of real respect for one another and mutual understanding.

These are some of the challenges that the Churches must face. They must do so constructively, openly and positively, as well as critically.

In order to look at this subject with some breadth of vision we offer first of all some remarks on the biblical and theological basis of freedom, justice and responsibility. We seek to do so in the light of the fact that in recent decades the Christian Churches in Ireland have grown in understanding of one another's beliefs and practices. That growth in understanding is an important step in the path towards the unity for which our Lord prayed (Jn 17:21). We seek, therefore, to look together at some at least of the main challenges which face us in our land today.

Freedom, justice and responsibility each reflect an aspect of the nature of God as seen in his action in the Old Testament in Israel and in the New Testament in Jesus Christ by the Holy Spirit.

I

ASPECTS OF FREEDOM

Freedom in the Old Testament is seen in relation to the God of Israel, manifest as the one true God who created free persons and the cosmos out of nothing and who, in turn, redeems people from bondage to serve him in liberty and peace. This gift was not given by nature, since it exceeds anything of which our nature is capable; it is a gracious gift of God. Because we are sinners it comes as a gift not only of divine generosity but also of forgiveness. The period which most closely embodies this is the Exodus event where God acted to deliver Israel from slavery, set the people free and led them to a new land and a better life. To disobey God meant to lose one's true freedom and receive judgement. This happened repeatedly in the history of Israel. Freedom in the Old Testament had also a communal context and was seen as comprehensive – for the whole of life, religious, social and political.

In the New Testament it is Christ by the Spirit who sets people free to become children of God. The freed person of the New Testament is contrasted with a slave (1 Cor 7:21f; Gal 3:23ff) but paradoxically the slave may become a freed person belonging to Christ and the freed person may become a slave of Christ. This freedom is not licence nor a merely legalistic concept; it cannot be received except by faith. It implies deliverance from a state of bondage to sin and evil. It also brings with it the reception and practice of forgiveness and moral imperatives to right and holy living. As in the Old Testament, it reaches out to a more social and political liberation (Lk 4:18; cf. Is 61). In most contexts it also implies an eschatological hope (Rom 8:19 ff).

Theological implications

The first of these is that freedom is an attribute of God as he really is. It can only be expressed on the basis of the revelation he has given us of himself in Jesus Christ by the Holy Spirit. That he reveals himself fully is an expression of his freedom. In this way we know he has the fullness of life and love in himself as Father, Son and Holy Spirit. In his triune freedom God is not solitary nor aloof but sets a pattern of all true freedom by being in relationship as Father, Son and Holy Spirit who are by, with, for and in one another. In other words his freedom is a differentiated, relational one, which has in it life, dynamic, order and peace. This has profound implications for the way we relate to one another as persons, as Churches and as social and political groupings on this island.

In his freedom God created a cosmos and human beings on it distinct from yet related to and dependent upon him. There is here a combination of freedom and creativity – in comparison with other views an absolutely new idea. In his free choice he moved to be the God of humanity and so is not only self-related but is in fellowship with humanity and creation. In this way humankind bears his image and likeness. Creation, as Luther said[2], is grace, a free act of God not imposed upon him but freely bestowed as he brings something different from himself into being. 'We believe that it [creation] proceeds from God's free will'.[3] In doing so he claims sovereign Lordship over creation. This is not an abstract ability to be or do anything; it is no arbitrary power, but a freedom determined by his loving nature, by the perfections made known to us in his revelation.

Divine freedom is exercised also in the further act by which God came in Jesus Christ to reconcile the world, freeing it from sinfulness and from opposition to him. This is expressed as free grace, as gospel, focused in the incarnation, death and resurrection of Jesus Christ. It is the freedom of victorious good news which reflects and conveys the very gracious freedom of life in which the triune God exists. In other words, in the actions of God in creation and reconciliation we have an expression of his freedom as he really is as our God. Knowledge of this freedom is thus not a human discovery but the result of God's action in Jesus Christ by the Holy Spirit.

Human freedom

Human freedom is the gift of God and has two aspects. The first is the natural freedom all have as creatures limited to space and time and free to make certain decisions for themselves, for others and for their environment. Ultimately these decisions are all subject to the overriding good will and purpose of God. The limited freedom of the creature is, however, seriously questioned and perverted by the reality of sin which takes away the will and ability properly to do the good and so be truly free. In other words, while sin brings us into bondage this creaturely freedom is never utterly set aside. It does, however, exist only within the wider context and overarching nature of the freedom bestowed by God in Jesus Christ.

Christian freedom is therefore that which God has made available for us in the reconciliation of Jesus Christ. It is, as we have seen, something given to us – by its very nature a divine gift. We cannot merit or earn it; it is something we receive. Its opposite is an act of unfreedom, of sin. Christian freedom is experienced further, as God's adoption of us 'in Christ', that is, in the Son, knowing his fatherly love and care. It is thus not a solitary, merely personal, experience but a communal one where both solitary and personal aspects are each recognised, exercised and expressed. True freedom, corresponding to God's nature, is our being with and for one another. At the same time it must be personally appropriated and received by faith resulting in the fruits of the Spirit, the good works of faith. In other words, the basic attitude and experience of freedom is affirmative, not negative.[4] Failure to know and receive the freedom of God does, however, mean the opposite of grace, namely, the experience of the judgment of God.

The view expressed above can be largely affirmed by the main Churches although its language is more typical of the Reformation than of Catholic theology. The former did not have a wholly uniform perception but a variety of expression at this point.

Differences in this area were fundamental to the divisions at the Reformation. Closer contacts have achieved a much greater level of mutual understanding on these issues.[5] Differences continue, nevertheless, to have their effect, not least in popular conceptions and misconceptions.

Catholic theology speaks of two freedoms, that of God to create new things, and the real though utterly dependent freedom of humans to work with or against God. In this view our present human freedom is fallen freedom which needs the grace of God. Alone our human freedom falls into slavery. Prevenient grace is offered to enable the human person to assent to redemption. Freedom is thus healed and restored. This view of the fall is of human freedom being 'wounded'; the Reformation thinks rather of freedom being 'destroyed'. This 'marks the deepest difference between the Catholic notion of grace, freedom and that of the Churches of the Reformation'.[6]

Such differences clearly have consequences for how one understands human participation in the freedom of God in his redeeming acts. It also influences how we perceive the freedom of God himself, his act of atonement and the place of merits and works in human redemption. In Catholic thought the human subject has a greater place than in the understanding of the Reformers and a slightly more optimistic view of human nature pertains in this conception of freedom.

There is also a differing popular conception and under-standing which is often reflected in diverse cultural forms. The particular view of people at the local parish level is sometimes at variance with stated Church belief and is assimilated to an extent to the cultural ethos of the times as well as influencing and conditioning it. This often results in various forms of mythology and can only be overcome by the actual truths the Churches seek to proclaim and embody being clearly presented to all. To gain freedom from mythology and freedom for the truth is a task for the Churches in relation to their members and society.

Practical implications

Freedom as grace and gospel
The Good News is that God sets us free in Christ his Son for himself, for love, worship and service. The need here is for personal and corporate repentance on the part of people both North and South – a conversion not only in people's personal lives but conversion to new attitudes and relationships which would begin to overcome our hatreds, our bitterness and our misunderstandings and transform our lives and the landscape of our society.

To do so one needs the reality of repentance, forgiveness and love. These have been set out clearly in various documents from member Churches. One Catholic document[7] looks forward to the end of the second millennium and underlines repentance (metanoia) as 'the precondition for reconciliation' (32) with God on the part of both individuals and communities. It recognises the fact of past actions being wrong, in fact being 'forms of counter-witness and scandal' (33). It instances 'intolerance and even the use of violence in the service of the truth' (35). These wrong attitudes in the past were a disservice to the unity willed by God for his people (34) and only repentance can bring a new way of forgiveness and reconciliation.

The Presbyterian Church[8] agreed at its General Assembly in 1965 to call upon its members to repent in the light of the scriptural message. It stated that its people should 'humbly and frankly acknowledge and ask forgiveness for any attitudes and actions towards our Roman Catholic fellow-countrymen which have been unworthy of our calling as followers of Jesus Christ' (22). It also called upon all its members 'to resolve to deal with all conflicts of interest, loyalties or beliefs always in the spirit of charity rather than of suspicion and intolerance and in accordance with the truth set forth in scripture' (22).

In 1994, as part of its response to the Opsahl Commission, the Methodist Church commented, 'If we genuinely want to put the past behind us, we must face up to the events of the past and accept our part of the responsibility for what has happened. The logic is also apparent – we must then strive to prevent those hurts, grievances and injustices from occurring again.'

These approaches are typical of the member Churches of the Irish Inter-Church Meeting at their best and have a vital part to play in bringing us nearer to the unity of Christ's Church and to freedom, justice and peace in Ireland as a whole. However, we must also openly admit that we have all failed in many ways to practise what we preach.

In this decade of evangelism the challenge is so to proclaim the good news of Jesus Christ that people will receive it, will be released from bondage to sin and set right with God and with one another. This is our mission as followers of Christ and at the same time it is the best counter to the negative aspects of secularism and to the licence which wrecks people's lives.

Freedom as communion – the Church
Since God is Father, Son and Holy Spirit, a free Being in relationship, his action towards us creates a community which reflects his nature. This is seen in the fellowship of the Church which is no self-realised, isolated phenomenon but a corporate body of believers – one, holy, catholic and apostolic. These four marks of the Church are each expressions of its freedom to be by, with and for one another:

one – an ecumenical vision and goal of unity;
holy – wholeness in the image of God;
catholic – universality, continuity, identity;
apostolic – mission and ministry in Christ's name.

While all affirm these marks as belonging to the true Church at the same time they are given by the different Churches connotations which divide and which, up to the present, have prevented and still hinder full unity and freedom. Each of us, however, traces our freedom to the same creative and redeeming acts of God's freedom.

Freedom as gift and task – some conclusions
The gift of freedom is a gift of God's forgiveness, freeing us from sin. Unwillingness to forgive is, therefore, inconsistent with welcoming the gift and grace of freedom. While the one who has offended another human being may never demand forgiveness as a right, willingness to forgive is nonetheless an obligation in one who has been forgiven by God (cf. Mt 18:22-35).

The gift of freedom is liberating because it frees us from the fear that life is absurd. Freedom is not a curse which obliges us to take part in a hopeless, ruthless battle in which everyone must look out for him or herself. It is an invitation to join with all humankind in trusting the providence of God who is love.

At the same time, the gift of freedom gives no ground for complacency. The merciful love of God calls for a response on our part by which we love God with all our heart and soul and might, and our neighbour as ourselves.

Questions

1. What can the Churches, together or singly, do to counteract the shallow secularism which does not recognise the free grace which is the foundation of Christian freedom? How can we increase understanding of the respect due to that gift and the obligations it brings?

2. The gift of freedom is offered to us in community. A choice which rejects or ignores the freedom of another person damages one's own freedom. Can the Churches do more to help people to understand that failure to respect the freedom of other individuals and groups can amount to a failure to appreciate the grace of God?

3. In situations of grave injustice and profound loss, willingness to forgive may seem an impossible ideal. (In practice, of course, actual forgiveness can only be given and received when it is sought and accepted.) What can be done to support people who have suffered great loss or injury in the painful struggle to achieve this ideal? How can people on both sides of the Northern Ireland community who have made that painful journey help one another?

II
ASPECTS OF JUSTICE

The terms justice, righteousness and justification are well known within the different theological traditions. They go back to the God known in Israel, the God of righteousness, who acts justly and vindicates his own righteousness. These terms are virtually synonymous with his saving acts. They imply a holiness in the people of the thrice holy God, corresponding to his holiness, and consequently a just ordering of society and a condemnation of all injustice.

Justice (or righteousness) is not, in the first instance, a human virtue but a gift from God; it is to be understood as a relational term. It is first of all a quality of God which becomes ours as we receive it in our fellowship with him. In political life it means doing right to all with mutual respect and commitment to others. This is particularly so in relation to the weak, the poor, the widow and orphan, the needy and oppressed. The social order is corrupted and people deprived of justice when wealth is wrongly accumulated and used as an instrument of power to exploit and oppress. Only a just ordering of society corresponds to the requirement of a righteous God. This is written into his covenant relationship with his people and the varied requirements this entails. No amount of sacrifice, however valid and necessary, avails if justice and right relationships are broken. God acts always to re-establish justice when it is set aside. He exercises judgment. It is a judgment, however, which operates within the perspective of a salvation involving righteousness, order and peace.

In the New Testament God justifies the sinner, exercises forgiveness in Christ and cleanses from all unrighteousness (I Jn 1:9). The link between justice and forgiveness brings out the fact that behind the whole righteousness group of words is a concept of relationship. The focus is on the concrete relationships of partners to each other. Thus the phrase the 'righteousness of God' becomes an expression for the unity of God's judging and redeeming acts. Justification, which sets the sinner right with God, has its parallel in right relationships with others, personally, corporately and in the context of society and political life.

At the same time it offers a critique of all worldly orders (*Magnificat*; Lk 2:12 ff) and hints at reversal of the social order of this world (Lk 16:19 ff). While the New Testament is less explicit than the Old when speaking of justice in social and political terms it nonetheless (together with the Old) forms the basis for our understanding of the nature of justice and righteousness.

Theological implications

Justice, righteousness and justification are in biblical understanding dynamic rather than static terms. Protestantism has tended to regard justification as being a status of right relations with God and in the Catholic tradition justification means both an act of God and the effect of being made right with God. Generally it is viewed today in active terms. This indicates the nature of God in his action towards sinners and a fallen world. He moves to set right what is wrong, to bring people into right relationship with himself and with one another. This he does in an exercise and act of costly grace in atonement where he himself in his Son acts rightly, offers to God the perfect righteousness which is his due. In the atonement of Christ he enables us to be freely just and righteous. This again is known and received by faith.

Justification and justice

The Catholic view recognises four stages in the experience of justification.[9] First, there is the prevenience of grace which goes before, preparing individuals for justification, and which involves a free assent of the person. Second, true faith is evoked when a person is made right with God by grace, justified by faith which is formed by love. This comes through the Church and baptism. Third, a person so justified is at the same time sanctified by co-operating with grace and by this meritorious activity being a true subject in salvation. Finally, there is both the possibility of losing one's status as justified and being reinstated but there is no real, definitive assurance of ultimate salvation. Justification always has an eschatological aspect pointing to the future judgement of God.

The Reformation tradition affirms that grace is the reality and offer of the mercy and forgiveness of God through the atoning work of Christ received by faith. In this understanding, by contrast, justification means that the sinner is declared righteous before God for the sake of Christ's righteousness. Sins are thus forgiven and the person is set in a process of being made holy (sanctification). This is sometimes spoken of as a 'two-fold grace'[10] by which the Holy Spirit unites us with Christ in a movement involving the declaratory act of justification and the beginning of a continuing process of sanctification. The two are distinguishable, the latter beginning with but following on the former. This twofold grace is received by faith alone which apprehends the love of God, and results in good works which are in no way meritorious in themselves. Such a justification is not revoked and is the basis for the assurance of ultimate salvation.

Clearly there is much in common between the two views. Indeed, within some of the Reformed Churches there is considerable sympathy both with the concept of prevenient grace and with what O'Grady, writing from a Catholic stance, calls co-operation and sub-operation. Nevertheless between Catholic and Reformed thought a somewhat different view of salvation, liberation and righteousness emerges. How far this leads to different conceptions in ethical, social and political life, is an open but real question. That it does so can scarcely be doubted.

Practical implications

1. *The link between faith and justice*

It is important to understand the close links between faith and justice. Our common faith summons us to value and respect our neighbour as ourselves.

It is impossible to pray genuinely if at the same time one regards oneself as superior to others (Lk 18:10-14). Before the infinite God we are all equal.

Recognition of equal dignity frequently requires as a first step that we become genuinely aware of the other's situation. Awareness of what it is really like to be unemployed or homeless is often quite lacking among those who have no direct experience of it. Such lack of understanding may exist even among members of one worshipping congregation.

The Churches have members who live in all possible situations, ranging from considerable affluence to grinding poverty. Many clergy in the course of their life's work will have lived among people of very different social backgrounds. The creation of genuine awareness of the other person, which is the first step in a genuine response, must be an important challenge to the Churches. It is a challenge which needs to be addressed both within individual congregations and between congregations.

Justice has to be more than a cold calculation of rights and duties. In a situation like Northern Ireland's, with genuine grievances in both communities, the building of justice needs more. It requires the self-sacrifice of those who refuse to retaliate, who will break the cycle, who are ready to forgive, who will stand for what is right even at the risk of rejection. It is faith which inspires witness.

Faith sees justice as a gift. God's justice is greater than any possible human achievement, greater than any human mind can imagine. God's justice is for all. Only God can give the justice for which we long, a justice which can embrace even those who are beyond the reach of our efforts.

2. The social and political spheres

If we are in a right relationship with God through faith in Jesus Christ and united with him by the Holy Spirit, this implies and brings about a righteousness in us personally.

In the **social sphere** if God sets us in relationships with himself in the Church and with one another this has consequences for life in society. This is now generally seen as having a trinitarian basis.[11] It excludes a narrow individualism (though it does value each human person) and sees people as social beings. 'A society is a group of persons bound together organically by a principle of unity that goes beyond each one of them.'[12] Society is not an abstract entity but a living community of people bound together in life to work for the common good. A great variety of social forms is possible and right but only those which create and allow true freedom and foster right relationships are just. They will act with justice for all, oppose oppression and injustice, care for the needy, the weak, the dispossessed, the voiceless and the poor in society. An ordering of society which does not include these and treats people contrary to these principles must be regarded as unjust.

No one form of freedom and justice is sacrosanct; only those which promote right relations and a just ordering of society and seek the greatest good of all are such. That which promotes community and good relationships should be the vision of the Churches. In our situation, both North and South, the need is to tackle the ills that beset us in unemployment, poverty, unjust structures and the various evils that stem from these wrongs.

In the **political sphere** we believe in common that the powers that be are of God, that each State exercises its authority from him. Every human community needs a rule which seeks to give freedom and justice to all and to promote responsibility. Such power is exercised under God and subject to his judgment. Where anyone is treated with injustice or where the order of political life and structures excludes rather than includes or discriminates against others (especially minorities) this is a situation that is evil.

No form of political structure is perfect but democratic institutions offer the best hope of political stability and just treatment of all. People matter most but structures are important since they either enable and expand freedom and justice or encroach upon both. It is particularly necessary in a land where there are divided communities and minorities with different ideologies that all be treated with fairness and impartiality. There must be an attempt to seek a solution for our problems where the word compromise is not regarded as wrong or as a sign of weakness but where it leads to conciliation, an accommodation of different allegiances, and commands the consent of the vast majority of people both North and South.

One can sum all this up by saying that the Lord requires that we do justly, love mercy and walk humbly with him (Mic 6:8). This includes opposition to social injustice and implies righteousness in society and in the political ordering of the State. Justice in our context in Ireland has therefore these twin foci. It enables, firstly, a just society which will be ordered for the benefit of all and, secondly, political structures that will give the greatest possible justice and freedom to all in the context of our divided loyalties. In all this people and personal relationships predominate but these should not be dissociated from structures that embody right relations, attitudes, social solidarity and political consensus.

Questions

1. The biblical witness links justice and forgiveness as two aspects of God's righteousness. To what extent do Christians, made righteous by God, manifest such a linkage in political and social discussion and/or structures? What concrete ways of living and acting flow from a concern for justice? Can there be justice without forgiveness or forgiveness without justice?

2. Different understandings of justification and its effects lead Christians to 'somewhat different view(s) of salvation, liberation and righteousness'. To what extent would common Christian action for justice be enhanced by deeper awareness of these different understandings of justification? Does the search for confessional agreement have any bearing on inter-denominational work for justice?

3. 'In the political realm we believe in common that the powers that be are of God, that each State exercises its authority from him'. Is this a fair statement of Christian belief and/or hope? Is it an expression of vision or of reality? What implications would this belief or hope have for Christians involved in the peace process? Are there significant differences among us about the role which it is appropriate for the State to exercise in fostering justice and truth in human relationships?

4. Our vision leads to an imperative to live as just people in a just society. How could the comments under **Practical Consequences** be made more concrete in order to address and challenge those seeking guidance or advice from the Churches?

III

ASPECTS OF RESPONSIBILITY

The term responsibility is scarcely mentioned in the Scriptures but nonetheless is implied in the whole thrust of the Bible message. The basic idea which underpins human responsibility in the Scriptures is the covenant of God with humankind, a covenant of grace freely instituted by him, expressed in his love and fidelity, and requiring the answer of lives lived in holiness and gratitude, with a faithfulness corresponding to that of God. In the Old Testament this is seen in the requirements God makes of his people, requirements which were so often unfulfilled.

In the New Testament the whole idea of responsibility is deeply embedded in the message and ministry of Jesus and in the preaching of the early Church. In the former it is chiefly associated with the Synoptic theme of the kingdom of God which is both 'from above' and at the same time is to be seen in the actions and attitudes of people in this world as they seek to fulfil the requirements of the kingdom. The new age that is dawning in the coming of Christ issues in a community of faith, hope and love where all have responsibilities not only to God but to one another, to their neighbours and to the world. This responsibility is chiefly summed up in love. At the same time one is held responsible for one's own wrong deeds. This responsibility is seen in the crucifixion of Jesus, by the Jews and Gentiles alike, the guilt for which can only be cleansed by the atoning work of Christ.

Responsibility is also seen in the whole ethical thrust not only of the teaching of Jesus but of later New Testament writings, in the fruits of the Spirit, in lives of holiness, and in the love, not only of one's neighbour, but of one's enemies.

Theological implications

The Bible speaks of God coming to act in the world of space, time and place, all of which in one sense he takes to himself. These are to be found in Israel and in God's acts through Israel to the Gentiles. They are seen in the coming of Christ to the land of Palestine, to the Jews, to a particular race and nation. Yet at the same time this particularity was never identified with any narrow nationalism; rather, enclosed within it is responsibility to all, to the total cosmos and all humanity. It has been called and is a concrete universal, radically calling into question all our conceptions of possessing, of being in time, space and place, yet, paradoxically, not denying these but affirming their validity.

The answer to this free grace of God is gratitude, the giving of oneself freely to a free God. In so acting one ventures oneself in obedience to the God who freely gives. 'It is the venture of responsibility in the presence of the giver and the fellow receivers of a gift, past, present and future.'[13] In this sense we are called to be partners, fellow workers with God and the community of his people and in witness and service to the world. This can only be accomplished where there is a free human act of response; obedience thus involves responsible behaviour in action with, for, before God and one's fellows. It can be expressed as a demonstration of our true humanity. It does not thus take us out of the world but in all our weakness and failure, sets us in it and brings us along the way God leads, making us his partners in the world.

Practical implications

Two of these are particularly relevant here.

1. The nature of authority

Since we are placed under God to serve, obey and reflect his nature, responsibility has aspects of submission to authority. Authority is an easily misunderstood word. The vision of the

Church requires the conception of rule as service, as the responsible use of love. It is ultimately the authority of grace, a grace shown in self-sacrifice. The idea, found in some modern discussion, that submission to God is contrary to freedom is a misunderstanding of the relationship of human freedom to God, 'Whom to serve is to reign'.[14] Submission to God, harmony with his will, is the purpose and the glory of human freedom. Freedom cannot be enhanced by a refusal to recognise the truth. God is not an external force among others, exercising pressure or influence. God is the source and giver of freedom.

There is a real difference between genuine *authority* which liberates and mere *power* which tends to dominate its subjects and to corrupt those who exercise it. Genuine authority is not an arbitrary imposition but is subject to the word and grace of God – in fact it embodies, exhibits and enables these.

The Church as the body of Christ is called and enabled to act in the spirit of service. While this is so, the Church must also have a shape and a ministry. Here again one must face the fact of different, and to some extent, opposing conceptions of what we generally call Church order – Episcopal, Congregational, Presbyterian, Papal – all with some (more or less) hierarchical structures. To see and enable these to serve the liberty of the children of God and of the world is a major task, challenge and responsibility which involves honest reflection on the nature of ministry and on how far our divisions impede the goals we set for ourselves.

2. The place of freedom and tradition

Each Church has its own particular tradition received from the past and related to freedom. Some even speak of 'The Tradition' as if it were a common heritage – which in some respects it is. In the 'Catholic' view tradition is a God-given guidance by which the Holy Spirit leads people into the truth of Christ which sets us free. Freedom is possible within this context of this truth.

The teaching of the Catholic Church is a complex and nuanced one. In the past Scripture and Tradition were largely seen by the Council of Trent[15] as twin sources to be received with 'equal respect of reverence and piety'. Vatican II spoke, however, of one source of authority in the revelation of God in Jesus Christ. This is encapsulated in the Tradition which 'comes from the Apostles and hands on what they have received from Jesus' teaching and example and what they learned from the Holy Spirit'.[16] Put otherwise, the living Tradition is embodied in 'the Church [which] in her doctrine, life and worship, perpetuates and transmits to every generation all that she herself is, all that she believes'.[17] In other words Tradition is the whole life of the Church in so far as it is engaged in handing on the faith to new generations.

Two main aspects of this are evident. They are to be seen as one, though distinguishable:

> Sacred Tradition and sacred Scripture make up a single sacred deposit of the Word of God which is entrusted to the Church... But the task of giving an authentic interpretation of the Word of God whether in its written form or in the form of Tradition has been entrusted to the living teaching office of the Church alone (Magisterium). Its authority in this matter is exercised in the name of Jesus Christ. Yet this Magisterium is not superior to the Word of God, but is its servant. It teaches only what has been handed on to it... It is clear, therefore, that in the supremely wise arrangement of God, sacred Tradition, sacred Scripture and the Magisterium of the Church are so connected and associated that one of them cannot stand without the others.[18]

At the same time the Catholic Church recognises what might be called lesser traditions which are developed in the handing on of the tradition: 'Tradition is to be distinguished from the various theological, disciplinary, liturgical or devotional traditions, born in local churches over time. In the light of Tradition these traditions can be retained, modified or even abandoned under the guidance of the Church's Magisterium'.[19]

Within the Churches of the Reformation there is some variety of approach. All will stress that the Holy Scriptures of the Old and New Testaments are the only rule of faith and practice and the supreme standard of the Church. However, those within, or close to, the Anglican tradition also accord special importance to the witness and practice of the early Church. All Reformed Churches would agree that the Scriptures are to be read in the context of the Church and interpreted by the Church as a whole, especially by its teachers and leaders. None, however, would see these as having the sole authentic right to interpret the Scriptures. Anglicans will stress the paramount importance of the writings and practice of the primitive Church in interpreting the Bible. Others will adopt what Karl Barth termed a 'respectful freedom in relation to tradition'.[20]

Though the Scriptures are written by human hands, they are nonetheless, through the work of the Holy Spirit, the Word of God as no other word ever written. To it no other writings are to be added; the Scriptures are necessary, sufficient and reliable, revealing Jesus Christ the living word. Here past traditions are treated with great respect but are subject to correction under the Word of God in Holy Scripture. In this sense freedom means the possibility of being liberated from one-sided or even erroneous teaching of the past in a Church seeking continual reformation. In a different way and with its own perspectives this was also attempted at Vatican II.

One should add here that in relation to the past there is a need not only to remember what has happened, to see where we have been, but to look to the future goal of our endeavours. We all require not only continuity with the past but the discontinuity of forgiveness which overcomes past wrongs and establishes new relationships. This attitude towards our varied traditions, repentance for past wrongs and a willingness to undertake responsibly new endeavours for peace, freedom, righteousness and justice, are all aspects which are extremely relevant to our situation here today.

From one point of view the traditions of different communities should primarily be seen as sources of enrichment not only for their own members but also for others who come in contact with them. This can be true in many aspects where we learn from one another and have our understanding added to and furthered. At the same time in our divided Churches people often find it impossible to accept some traditions as possible enrichments since they cannot identify with or gain benefit from what they perceive as either lacking the fullness of the truth or as being in certain respects erroneous. Inter-church relations afford the opportunity for people to assess how far they can go together and learn from each other but they also show us the extent of the remaining differences.

Cultural traditions may be somewhat different since they are at a more human level. It is one of the aspects of the Irish scene that, while we experience different cultural views, many people come into close contact with 'the other tradition' only occasionally and may have hardly any significant encounters with foreign cultures. Whether our cultures can accommodate interchange so that people maintain their own views while benefiting from one another depends to a large extent on whether we see our cultures as open or as exclusive. The experience, for example, of Britain today with its inter-cultural, pluralistic society shows that there is much mutual reception of others' views but there are also groups which are very exclusive, where this enrichment does not follow. The same is to some extent true in our own land.

The mission given by Jesus to his followers was that they should make disciples of all nations (Mt 28:19). The Gospel is meant for every culture. There is no suggestion that new disciples should abandon their cultural heritage. The Gentile converts were not to be forced to accept the religious/cultural traditions of Judaism (Acts 15).

The unity of Christ's followers does not, therefore, imply a cultural uniformity. The kind of unity which would seek to blur all cultures into a false cosmopolitan sameness finds no justification in the Gospel.

Such a unity is, in any case, impossible. The sameness can only be achieved by driving differences in belief and values, differences in historical perceptions and experiences, underground as divisive or private, as irrelevant to public life, as never to be given public expression. It would require the attitude which the insight and irony of Jewish humour summed up in the phrase *incognito ergo sum.*[21] An attempt to create a tolerant, pluralist society on such a basis may in fact have the opposite effect. It can result in a situation where differences, because they are never publicly discussed, remain unacknowledged, badly understood and in practice divisive.

One measure of the health of any culture is its openness to the wider human culture, its ability to communicate, to learn from the riches of other cultures and to communicate to them its own riches. It is above all in that exchange that a people or a community can come to recognise what is limited or limiting, what is dead or dehumanising, what is sick or sinful, in its own institutions, attitudes and traditions. The vitality of a culture is seen in its ability to discern and learn from what is good in itself and in others, and in its ability to recognise and change what is evil.

The ethical imperative
Underlying this is an ethic of freedom, justice and responsibility. It can be stated in this way: The gift of the grace of God setting us free involves the task or responsibility of living out freedom and justice in the concrete circumstances of everyday life. The Germans put it that the *Gabe* (the gift) involves the *Aufgabe* (the task). As we have seen, while freedom is a gift, it is also at the same time composed of human acts and decisions. In the New Testament, beside the indicative stands the imperative which is

included in the gift of freedom. It is freedom to choose, to act rightly and responsibly before and in obedience to God and before and on behalf of one's fellows and creation. The commandments and requirements of the free God for his covenant partners come within the context of grace.

To this extent, while laws, commands and requirements are enjoined, they are to be seen as the answering response of the free person to the free God who seeks concrete, right, responsible decisions in very specific situations. Rules and laws in the Christian sense, as manifest in the Scriptures and in traditional ethics, give us guidelines but do not always set out instructions for every possible situation. Actions in free decision do not set aside the laws and commandments of God but see them as intended to be understood in the light of the liberating, redeeming acts of God and related to particular situations in which people find themselves. This is not 'situation ethics' but an ethic of freedom based on the will of the free God. Actions are thus regarded as free and morally right in so far as they correspond to the nature and purpose of God and are carried out in direct responsibility to him.

The Catholic view of the place of rules in morality is stated as follows: 'The commandments properly so called come in the second place. They express the implications of belonging to God through the establishment of the covenant. Moral existence is a response to the Lord's loving initiative. It is the acknowledgement and homage given to God and the worship of thanksgiving. It is co-operation with the plan God pursues in history.' [22]

At the same time the Catholic tradition insists on the importance of recognising that there are rules which admit of no exception. There are things which it is never right to choose to do, choices which are wrong in themselves. This insistence on the existence of universally binding norms does not ignore the problems about the precise formulation of such norms: 'There is a need to seek out and discover the most adequate formulation for universal and permanent moral norms in the light of different cultural contexts, a formulation most capable of ceaselessly expressing their historical relevance, of making them understood and of authentically interpreting their truth'.[23] In the end only a morality which acknowledges norms valid always and for everyone, a morality whose fundamental obligations apply equally to weak and strong can provide a foundation for 'just and peaceful human coexistence, and hence of genuine democracy, which can come into being and develop only on the basis of the equality of all its members.... Before the demands of morality we are all absolutely equal'.[24]

This can be put otherwise by saying that ethical actions are never taken in a vacuum even though they may be individual and personal choices. They relate to and impinge on others for good or ill. They involve challenge, correction and counselling as well as being challenged, corrected and counselled. They also have the character of a search by the individual in community, a seeking to find the will of God and the grace of knowing and doing it. It is both a divine task and service required of us by God and a human act of service in which one finds true freedom and righteousness.

One of the most recent agreed statements in the ecumenical dialogue is the Anglican-Roman Catholic International Commission (ARCIC) document entitled *Life in Christ.*[25] It sees Christian morality as the fruit of life in Christ by the Holy Spirit and received by faith. It thus goes back to the basic reality of the Gospel of grace – a common starting-point for the Churches which results in large areas of common ground in our understanding of the nature of morality and its practical expression in particular cases. It is agreed that 'all moral authority is grounded in the goodness and will of God' (49). While both communions share a common basis they differ in their conceptions of authority and how particular ethical issues are to be resolved. In Anglicanism authority is dispersed to allow for the greatest possible liberty whereas in Roman Catholicism a need for a central authority to preserve unity is essential (49).

A central thrust of the document is that both communions share not only a basic vision based on Holy Scripture but fundamental values that flow from this, for example the sanctity of human life, the goodness of God's original creation and the permanence of the marriage bond, among others. A distinction is made between these basic moral values and particular conclusions which are derived from them (63). There is a great degree of unity in the former but less in the latter, for example in marriage, divorce and contraception. Here differences of discipline and pastoral practice emerge (50). Roman Catholicism sees certain actions as intrinsically, objectively and morally wrong always (for instance, abortion). Anglicans, while upholding moral absolutes, see these more in relation to contextual and pastoral considerations (52).

The document is interesting in that it moves away from a moral conception largely based on law to one based on the Gospel, on the Scriptures and grace of God. The emphasis is on the Trinity and our correspondence to Father, Son and Holy Spirit, as persons in community. The moral values we have and seek to attain should reflect this being-in relationship of the triune God. 'The moral dimension is thus conceived as fundamentally relational' (52). This raises the further question of the right balance between regard for the person and regard for the institution. These are not contraries but are, rather, complementary.

The document notes that how to discern agreements and disagreements between the two communions is not always an easy task. Nonetheless, the practical conclusion to be drawn is that there is a direct, clear link between our disunity and our varied perceptions of how to relate morality to practical concerns. The positive side of this is that it is not only through our discussions of doctrine but also through those on morality that our common goal of Church unity and communion may be further advanced.

Questions

1. To what extent are differences between and within the Churches on moral questions related to differences in understanding of the basis of moral judgement? Are there differences, at least in emphasis, about the relative importance of Scripture, tradition and human reason in arriving at moral conclusions? Are there differences in the understanding of conscience?

2. 'The primacy of persons is emphasised above the impersonalism of a system of law, thus avoiding the distortions – of both individualism and utilitarianism' (*Life in Christ*, ARCIC, no. 52). One reason why it can be difficult to discuss moral issues is that people operate out of moral philosophies which lead to distortions – individualism, utilitarianism and legalism. Would it be helpful if the Department of Theological Questions were to look in some depth at these different approaches and attempt to outline an approach to these issues which would do justice to the richness of human and Christian freedom?

3. How far may differences of approach among the member Churches be related to different views about the possibility/ desirability/necessity of formulating universally binding norms which admit of no exception? Is the underlying agreement among Christians about the sanctity of life – for instance in relation to abortion – weakened by this disagreement?

4. How far do different approaches to the appropriate legal expression of 'social issues' such as divorce and abortion relate to different understandings of authority? How far do they arise from different understandings of the role of the State? Would it be helpful to understand more clearly the root of such differences, even if they cannot be resolved?

IV
PLURALITY AND TRUTH

Pluralism is a difficult term to define and describe. One view is that it is the accommodation of different opinions, ideologies, creeds and values within the overarching framework of a society where all can live with and tolerate each another. More frequently, however, the term is associated with a view which denies that there can be any objective truth in the area of religious beliefs and values and strongly disapproves of such an idea as intrinsically divisive. The result, from a Christian perspective, is a form of relativism and reductionism. In the Scriptures there are 'gods many and lords many' but only one true God, the God of Israel revealed in his fullness in his Son Jesus Christ and in the Holy Spirit.

Theological implications

While, in some ways, the early Church was less legalistic than Judaism and more accommodating in relation to others, at the same time it strongly affirmed the sole Lordship of Christ in life and conduct (e.g. I Cor 8:5, 6; Eph 6:5-9). He was and is the answer to the question of truth(e.g Jn 1:14; 14:6). In him we have the final, complete revelation of God. Christians sought to live by this truth and witness to it, to do so without violence and simply by testimony and persuasion.

In the realm of social conduct and education the nascent Christian Church showed an open-mindedness to the surrounding society which could be described in one sense as pluralistic.

In the realm of values and beliefs, however, they had a robust confidence in the truth which they proclaimed, believing that it was God's Word to a needy world. Truth was not a matter of personal choice between equally valid alternatives. Truth was absolute because it had been revealed by God at a particular time in history through a particular figure, Jesus Christ. The absolute nature of that truth is clear in the apostolic preaching (e.g. Acts 4:11, 12) as it is, for instance, in the Johannine community (I Jn 2:22, 23; 3:23).

Believing firmly in that truth, they went out to tell the good news to others and to persuade them of the truth. They would certainly not have conformed to the Shorter Oxford Dictionary's definition of pluralism as 'a system of thought which recognises more than one ultimate principle'. It must be stressed, however, that they never had the desire nor the means to compel anyone to come to their way of thinking. John and Paul both stress that people have a responsibility to respond to the light, but neither gives grounds for any suggestion that they should be compelled. Such behaviour was unfortunately practised by many later Christians.

Practical implications

Our inter-church situation cannot be described as a pluralistic one if that word is used in the sense of denying any absolute standard. While our expression of it varies, we all claim to have an understanding of the truth of God and Christ. Some regard others' views as erroneous or incomplete in detail if not *in toto*. None of us regards the truth as unimportant or relative. The pluralism that denies the absolute transcendent, that knows no objective centre of life, is, from the Christian point of view, unacceptable. The Christian vision of pluralism in society is not to be seen as a reluctant and half-hearted version of a full-blown relativism.

The modern disillusionment with ideologies and systems reveals a flaw at the heart of the attempt to build a society which sees no need for any transcendent truths or values. What C. S. Lewis called the 'hideous strength' of ideologies lies in their inability to recognise the hollowness of their position. The extreme and totalitarian movements of this century are driven by an immovable will to transform the human condition, but they lack any deep understanding of what it means to be human:

> An acknowledgement of the incapacity of liberal democracy to provide and foster its own moral foundations is urgently needed. [26]

The challenge of living in a modern society is to learn to live in harmony with people whose religious and philosophical approach to the moral foundations differs from one's own. That kind of social harmony is a most desirable goal in Ireland. It involves recognising the importance and the sacredness of the human search for the truth and deep respect for the efforts of each individual and group to seek the truth. In Ireland, in the past, and in the present, people have sought to impose their ideologies, their beliefs and their political opinions on others, often with violence. At the same time some have discriminated against others on grounds of religion, culture and values.

The pluralism which denies any absolute standard is mistaken not because it is too respectful of the opinions of every person but because it is not respectful enough. A person's honest convictions are worthy of the greatest respect, not because the outcome of the search for truth is unimportant but because it is of the utmost importance. The human quest for understanding of what is true and good and beautiful is, in its deepest significance, the search for the Creator of all.

An approach which would say, in effect, 'Believe what you like, it is no concern of mine', is not compatible with a firm belief in the truth of the Gospel and a deep respect for the individual's search for meaning, a search with culminates in the God who comes out to meet us.

This implies an approach where human search meets God's coming. When the relationship between God and humankind is seen as God's coming fully into our humanity in Jesus Christ, the Word Incarnate, it follows that in him both the coming and the search are one. The search is thus to be understood in the light of the incarnation as faith seeking understanding, since the truth is something given. When one speaks of the truth in the Church's understanding one means the reality of a personal act of disclosure by God and a meeting with him. Truth is not, therefore, something abstract or merely conceptual.

Respect for the individual's search for truth does not mean that one may never express disagreement. It would be wrong for society to seek to coerce people into acting against their convictions; it does not follow that a society should never show a preference for one lifestyle or one kind of behaviour over another:

> What justifies the reinforcement of preferences is the realization that there is no possibility of neutrality. The failure to publicly endorse these goals [life-long marriage, the importance of independent centres of learning, the value of voluntary associations] is tantamount to asserting their unimportance.[27]

The path to harmony in a society which contains different cultural and religious traditions does not lie in the avoidance of contact but in the deepening of mutual knowledge:

> How can the culture which is predominant in a given society accept and integrate new elements without losing its own identity and without creating conflicts? The answer to these difficult questions can be found in a thorough education with regard to the respect due to the consciences of others; for example through greater knowledge of other cultures and religions, and through a balanced understanding of such diversity as already exists.[28]

It might be argued that the growth of liberalism in the last century was possible only because, 'it was able to take for granted a high degree of shared morality and belief... The problem is that pluralism gives rise to deep and intractable conflicts while at the same time undermining the principles by which they might be resolved. It disintegrates our concept of the common good'.[29]

'The more plural a society we become, the more we need to reflect on what holds us together.'[30]

It would be a real loss if, in the name of pluralism, it became impossible to consider and discuss the ultimate grounding of our systems of law (whether constitutional law or common law) and the basis for decisions about the laws and structures under which we live. We need to be able to consider together the answers to basic questions about the purpose for which the State exists if our society is not to become fundamentally incoherent. It would be a mistake to think that the way in which a political, judicial or economic system functions can be understood without reference to its history, its intellectual presuppositions, its 'sacred texts' and its religious role.

It would be a real loss if, in the name of pluralism, our systems of education were to adopt an approach which presented all faiths in a merely objective way and did not provide young people with the opportunity to grow in knowledge of their own tradition. 'The problem is that giving many religions equal weight is not supportive of each but tends rapidly to relativise them all.'[31]

Questions

1. How can the Churches work together in the building of a more tolerant society? What more might be done in the area of fostering growth in understanding? How might we encourage a move from merely passive tolerance to positive interest in and respect for the religious beliefs and cultural heritage of others?

2. How might the Churches work together to show that real pluralism does not imply a denial of the objectivity of truth? Can we increase understanding of the fact that a recognition of the importance of a person's search for truth is the foundation of genuine pluralism?

3. Is there more that the Churches could do to show that, when people recognise that their religious beliefs, moral standards or cultural traditions are different, this need not be 'divisive'? Can we help to show that, on the contrary, it is the path to better mutual understanding?

V

HOPE FOR PEACE

The Christian faith knows God as a God of hope. That hope is based on the person and work of Christ and particularly on his resurrection from the dead. This is the basis of a sure hope for fellowship with God here and now and for the life eternal. It is a hope which affects our present lives and society and creates a spirit of confidence, watchfulness, expectancy and prayer. This future dimension is a factor in determining our present as is the reality of our past.

In one sense the end times have come in Jesus Christ; in another they are the object of future hope. This enables Christian people to endure affliction, violence, turmoil, wars and rumours of wars with courage, steadfastness and vigilance. These qualities are not entirely lacking in those without such hope any more than they are all manifestly present in those who do have it. The Churches, while often failing in courage and vision, have nonetheless often been communities of hope and peace over the past twenty-five years.

This basis in our faith is one positive sign of our hope for peace. The other is that the God who has reconciled us to himself and calls a people to be one with each other, is the sovereign Lord of all. He can and does act when, where and as he pleases (*extra muros ecclesiae*). The New Testament speaks of a *Kairos* centred and based on the Christ events but these events have at the same time universal significance and validity. In this light, while God speaks and acts primarily through his appointed means – the Bible, the sacraments and prayer – it is possible to recognise (on the basis of his once-for-all unique revelation) his works in the world – even to be able, sometimes, to call these 'miracles'. Human beings may be his agents but his is the hand that guides and the will that purposes change and gives hope and peace. In the biblical drama Cyrus (2 Chron 36:22ff.) and others outside the people of God were clearly his instruments. He acts not only through the Churches but in the world.

In our world we have seen the hope of peace and great changes for good take place in the former Soviet Union and its satellites, in South Africa and in the Middle East. However, the examples mentioned above warn us that hope for peace can sometimes be a fragile thing and our situation is no exception. Real peace is not simply the absence of violence but the presence of new attitudes and relationships. That is not easy to achieve. Old animosities can easily be rekindled, even erstwhile friends and neighbours can destroy one another. The sin in all human beings weighs us down to impede progress.

The same holds true in our own land. The 'peace process', as it is called, offers signs of hope; it may be also hijacked and its content interpreted in a way that is one-sided and unbalanced. It can be turned into a propaganda weapon by one or several groups to be used against each other. The new opportunities that have been given to us may yet be squandered. Nonetheless, we must set before ourselves a vision of hope, a vision of peace without violence, of the lion lying down with the lamb, of people speaking peace one to another and, as the Scriptures put it, 'doing the truth'. At the same time we recognise the great obstacles to be overcome in a long history of opposition, hatred, armed struggle and opposed ideologies.

The attitude to be adopted towards our situation from the Christian perspective must, however, be a positive one that points to hope and a search for enduring peace with freedom, justice and responsibility. This moment, fraught though it is with many dangers, may be a *Kairos* of opportunity, to be seized, worked upon, prayed over, that God may lead us to accommodations of peace so that the future may be a day of righteousness, freedom and real peace in our land.

The biblical basis

The whole history of God's activity with and for humankind can be set out in terms of peace.

Old Testament

Peace (*shalom*) is expressed as well-being for humanity, coming ultimately from God and affecting every area of life.[32] It approximates closely to salvation. It is a gift of God; persons or a community that receive *shalom* are recipients of God's grace. It confers a quality of life and spirit transcending all earthly gifts, benefits or success. In later Old Testament passages (Mic 1, I K 25:5ff, Ezk 13:10,16) the true prophets expose the false who are discredited through their political machinations (Is 54:10). In turn the prophets point forward to a new age of righteousness and peace seen in terms of splendour, salvation and glory. They indicate the promise of a Prince of Peace bringing everlasting peace (Is 9:56). The final state will be that of universal reconciliation in nature, among the peoples, and between Israel and God.

Peace is always closely related to righteousness and obedience. The gift requires the task of seeking justice and right relationships.

New Testament

This continues and brings the Old Testament message to its fulfilment, is centred in the reign of God proclaimed in Jesus Christ and the reality of salvation he has brought by his life, death and resurrection. Salvation as wholeness brings peace and righteousness. Its basis is grace, God's act of redemption in Jesus Christ. In place of the disorder of human beings it establishes the order of divine righteousness which alone brings true well-being. In place of enmity and division between peoples and races, it brings reconciliation.

Peace as a form of God's revealed will has a trinitarian character:

1) It is centred in Jesus Christ who is our peace, breaking down the dividing walls between opposing, hostile groups and peoples and making the two one in the body of Christ by the cross. In this way through a costly atonement a new creation is brought about (Col 1:2; Eph 2:14-17).

2) It comes as the fruit of the Holy Spirit (Gal 5:22), who is the giver of life (Rom 8:6), the One who enables the unity of the Church to be maintained (Eph 4:13). As such it is an aspect of the Kingdom of God which inspires justice, peace and joy (Rom 14:17).

3) It is from God (the Father), the God of peace. The whole work of salvation is referred back to him; the resurrection, the eternal covenant in the blood of Christ (Heb 13:20), victory over Satan (Rom 16:20), sanctification and preservation till the Lord returns (I Thess 5:22).[33]

The peace that comes through Christ from the Father by the Holy Spirit is other than the world gives since it reflects the unity and community of the triune God. This gift of peace is both a victorious power in the present (Phil 4:7, Col 3:13) and the goal of the Christian's calling. It operates among people as harmony (Rom 14:19, I Cor 14:37, 2 Tm 2:22, Jm 3:18, I P 3:11). It is manifest in forgiveness and in a spirit of unity in the Church. We are to live at peace with all (Heb 12:14), as seen in right attitudes and relationships. Agreement and harmony at all costs are not envisaged; righteousness, however, is. If it is possible we are to live at peace but opposition to wrong may lead to temporary disharmony and lack of peace.[34] Peace is, therefore, always closely associated with truth and right, with freedom and responsibility. Peace sought at the expense of righteousness would be a false peace. The search for peace is an essential aspect of love for one's neighbour and one's enemy on the basis of God's love for us.

The New Testament has little to say directly about peace in the social and political sense but much of its ethical teaching has implications in these spheres. The only direct reference is

Matthew 5:9: 'blessed are the peacemakers'. This is given in the context of discipleship, that is, of grace, and it implies that Christ's followers are blessed if they build bridges between people, are peacemakers, doers of the word and as such show themselves to be children of God – the God of peace. Of considerable importance also is prayer which can be called a powerful political ingredient in any peace process. We are reminded to pray for all authorities that 'we may live a peaceable and quiet life in all godliness and holiness' (I Tm 2:2).

As one can see from this theological and ethical basis, peace cannot be perceived or pursued in isolation. In biblical thinking it is set in the context of God's reconciliation in Jesus Christ. It concerns the Church in particular but also the whole of humanity and the created order. It therefore relates to questions such as freedom and righteousness (justice).

With this biblical background we now look at three areas in more detail.

1. The Church and the Churches – unity and peace

Since God has united us in Jesus Christ, who is our peace 'through the blood of his cross' (Eph 2: 13, 14), and made former enemies 'one flesh', division within the Church is a denial of peace. The steps that have been taken and are being taken to realise the goal of unity and peace have at their heart the knowledge that this is in accordance with the will of God. The goal of unity is right; it offers the possibility of greater co-operation among the Churches in their witness to the world. While we remain either still divided or differing in faith we are a stumbling-block to peace and justice. Many factors contribute to this – some principled and others clearly based on misconceptions and prejudices. One cannot have peace and unity on the lowest common denominator or where some see others as making claims they cannot accept. Nor can one have unity and peace where a narrow vision obstructs progress and hinders dialogue.

The peace process of the Churches has been and is a difficult, sometimes rewarding but also often frustrating one with its periods of stagnancy or, worse still, of a retreat from many aspects of co-operation and dialogue here in Ireland. At the same time the vision cannot and must not be set aside since it is based on the grace of God and the assurance of his will for the Churches to be at peace with one another through unity with Christ. This vision enables us to participate in the continual task of the search for better co-operation, visible unity and true peace.

What present steps should be taken to make this vision a reality?

- Emphasis on the God-givenness of unity as the nature of the vision we have and the task we pursue.
- A realistic awareness of continuing doctrinal differences and an attempt to pursue further dialogue with the aim of greater co-operation and ultimate unity.
- A setting out of more immediate and possible, attainable goals as symbols and pointers to the ultimate goal and as signs of hope.
- The education of people in attitudes of peace, reconciliation, forgiveness and love which oppose all hatred, bitterness and attitudes that undermine unity and peace.

2. The context of peace

Peace is never an isolated phenomenon. It is set in a context of relationships, personal and communal. In the biblical view, as we have seen, it flows from God's grace. Grace and peace come to us in that order, the latter a consequence of the former (Eph 1: 2, Phil 1: 2, Col 1:2, etc.) Peace on earth to those on whom God's favour rests is seen in the light of God's glory (Lk 2: 14). Peace is at the cost of the sacrifice of Christ on the cross and is related to the righteousness of God. God has acted in Christ in atonement which means that broken relationships are healed between God and humanity, God and creation. The righteousness and holiness of God require an answering righteousness from us which we as sinners cannot give. Christ does this in our humanity, makes the perfect offering of righteousness by bearing God's judgment on our sins, freeing us to know forgiveness, righteousness and peace. We are justified by faith in his work and so set right with God and with one another. This action of God sends us in a different direction and results in new ways of righteousness and peace. Here again, we see peace in the context of other aspects of the faith, God's grace, his righteousness and Christ's atonement.

3. Peace, society and the political realm

God's righteous ways with us in setting wrong relations right have their parallels in the world involving justice in society and righteousness in the political order. Where there is no justice conflict ensues and disorder takes place.

a) *Society*

A peaceful and prosperous society can only flourish where all are treated with justice and parity of esteem. Where greed, acquisitiveness, selfishness and injustice predominate, society becomes corrupt through the idolatry of wealth, neglect of the poor, the underprivileged, abuse of children and women. The evil fruits of such a lack of justice in the social order are plainly set out in the Old Testament scriptures as well as the New. The result is decay, disintegration and judgment on all unrighteousness.

The Christian faith calls for a just society where neither wealth corrupts nor poverty destroys, but where real attempts are made to adjust imbalances, treat all people with fairness and generosity and so sow the seeds of a better way and good relations with all. How that is to be worked out in practice is a matter primarily for the State but also for some input from the Churches.

However, two indications point to a way of social justice.

1) The attempt to reflect God's character in human relations, following the way of love and holiness, right dealings and fair treatment given to all.

2) The thrust of the gospel is from above downwards – down to the needs of humanity and out to share resources with all and especially with the disadvantaged, the poor and vulnerable, both nationally and internationally. The popular option for the poor may not encapsulate this entirely, but the message of the gospel emphasises justice, and freedom and proclaims the words and works of Christ who acted for us all in being lowly and humble, sharing our need and taking away our sins by his life, death and resurrection.

The ideal is set out clearly in the following statements from two documents. The first, from Pope John XXIII, sums up many of our concerns.

> Before a society can be considered well-ordered, creative, and consonant with human dignity, it must be based on truth. St Paul expressed this as follows: 'Putting away lying, speak ye the truth every man with his neighbour, for we are members of one another' (Eph 4:25). And so it will be, if each man acknowledges sincerely his own rights and his own duties toward others. Human society, as we here picture it, demands that men be guided by justice, respect the rights of others and do their duty. It demands, too, that they be animated by such love as will make them feel the needs of others as their own, and induce them to share their goods with others, and to strive in the world to make all men alike heirs to the noblest of intellectual and spiritual values. Nor is this enough; for human society thrives on freedom, namely, on the use of means which are consistent with the dignity of its individual members, who, being endowed with reason, assume responsibility for their own actions.[35]

The second is part of a statement endorsed by the Presbyterian Church in Ireland at the General Assembly (1994).

> We believe that the same evangelical faith in Jesus Christ, which emboldens us to pray to God as our heavenly Father, challenges us to develop radically new attitudes and relationships with our neighbours in Ireland...

that to be Christian peacemakers in our own situation, we must grasp more clearly the distinctive teaching of our Lord which challenges the general practice of our world...

that we must encourage all efforts to establish new structures of consent and participation ...

that we must be initiators of programmes of action which will contribute to peace in our community ...
that peacemaking is an affirmation and accommodation of diversity...

The justice that flows from the reconciling words and work of Jesus Christ deals with social ills as well as spiritual and produces that righteousness which alone exalts a nation.[36]

b) *The political realm*

Peace flows also from proper political structures where freedom prevails and each section of society has a place and voice in the affairs of a nation and its people. Since all power and authority ultimately come from God, State authority owes its origin to him. It has a duty to establish a form of government that respects and furthers the rights of all, and in turn gains acceptance and respect from the citizens for its authority and policies. Every political regime is, however, relative and limited to the forms of this world.

The only absolute claim is God's claim and the only ultimate loyalty is due to God. When any political order transgresses the limits of the human and creaturely and makes absolute claims it is unjust, becomes oppressive and ends in conflict, not in peace. Peace can only be built on a society that respects just laws and order and has the consent of the people freely expressed and given to government.

Human freedom is interdependent. One person's abuse of freedom is another person's enslavement. Peace is the situation where everybody's freedom is respected. This has clear implications for the principle of consent.

When, as in Ireland, allegiances are given to different governments within the one land peace is more difficult to achieve. The history of our island home over the centuries bears witness to this. It has too often led to conflict rather than to co-operation and peace. The way of peace in this situation is not through armed conflict and violence. Recent events have shown the terrible, tragic and negative consequences of this in the loss of life, property and bitter opposition and in a polarisation of people in society. In looking back to the past we must remember above all the cost (which still continues) in human lives, broken hearts and sad homes where there has been great loss and sorrow. The 'peace process,' no matter what happens to it, is at least a first indication that the policy of violence has failed and a new, better way of peace must be found. As Churches, a prime duty for all is to be peacemakers and bridge-builders as we seek ways forward.

How then can one evaluate political proposals from a Christian perspective? The following are four suggested questions to be asked about any political proposals:

- Will they lead to better political structures for our island, and these islands as a whole?
- Will the main traditions and minorities accept them as a way forward which respects the interests of all, and with which they can, on the whole, identify?
- Has a proper balance been struck between the conflicting interests and ideologies, and do they, therefore, incorporate that justice which will secure peace and co-operation in the future?
- Will they lead to the complete cessation of all violence, North and South, and enable the formation of free, democratic institutions where compromise is seen not as betrayal, but as a way in which people can seek to understand and respect the other's point of view and make the necessary accommodations in righteousness and peace?

VI
CONCLUSION

One of the things that has emerged in this study and is in line with modern trends in theology is an emphasis on the central significance of personal relationships between individuals and communities, especially in the Church. God is conceived as 'being-in-relationship', the Father with the Son by the Holy Spirit, three persons in a fellowship of mutual self-giving love. Creaturely personhood is fully real as it participates individually and corporately in the life of the triune God. This is not to say that forms or institutions are set aside as unimportant. Many of these, such as scripture, Church and ministry, are divinely given means of grace by which people are enabled to share in the divine life and to answer the call of God to holy living in accordance with his purpose and to his glory. It is this holistic vision that underlies our thinking on freedom, justice and responsibility and, hopefully, makes it properly Christian.

It is this vision that allows us to speak of the hope for peace. Even where we do not see clearly how mutual respect and lasting peace can be achieved, the promise of *shalom* assures us that God's peace is all-inclusive. All those who belong to the eternal kingdom, whatever their differences of culture or even belief, will find there the fulfilment of their deepest hopes, the flourishing of their varied gifts. They will find all that is good in their cultural inheritance, transformed and glorified.

The fact that our plans are inadequate and our expectations limited is not a reason for despair. It is a reason for hoping in God whose folly is wiser than human wisdom and whose weakness is stronger than human strength.

PART TWO

THE REALITY OF
IRELAND TODAY

INTRODUCTION
AUDITING THE CHURCHES IN IRELAND

The Christian Church, in the sphere of social reality, has a twofold task which springs from its very nature: to combat injustice and bring about reconciliation. The struggle for justice, which is sustained by the Church's fundamental option for the poor and embraces both oppressors and oppressed, often involves conflict when the structures that perpetuate injustice must be challenged. This struggle is not specifically Christian unless it also leaves room for mutual forgiveness and enables parties to conflict to enter into each other's experience and point of view, thereby making reconciliation possible.[37] In taking this approach we are mindful of the documents of the Second Vatican Council (*Lumen gentium,* 1) and the World Council of Churches (Uppsala Assembly, I,20) which see the Church not only as the sacrament or sign of the coming unity of humankind, but equally as a sign of contradiction where the causes of disunity must be confronted. We are inspired as well by the theology of liberation which originated in the very different context of Latin America, and by the *Kairos Document* of the South African Churches, which insist that in its prophetic role the Church sometimes cannot avoid becoming involved in political conflict. We are convinced, however, that the Churches in Ireland have a specific contribution to make in stressing the necessity of mutual forgiveness if reconciliation is to be deep and lasting. Ireland's long preoccupation with constitutional issues, however, has meant that insufficient attention has been paid to poverty and pluralism in Irish society itself, to its class structure and its political evolution. In taking this approach, we are not speaking of a Church which stands separate from 'the world' as if this were alien to it, but a Church that is 'the world' in the process of transformation towards a form of life in Christ's image.

Our aim is to present a critique or audit of the effectiveness of the Churches in Ireland today in relation to key trends and issues on which freedom, justice and responsibility have a bearing. We will focus on three main areas:

1) the political issue, in particular the ongoing conflict in Northern Ireland;
2) the economic issue, in particular with respect to those who are disadvantaged;
3) the issue of pluralism.

Our audit does not claim to be exhaustive, but does aim to help the Churches identify areas in which their own contribution to society on the island of Ireland might be more in line with gospel values.

I

THE CHURCHES WITHIN THE POLITICAL SITUATION

The situation

It is right to begin by acknowledging the positive contribution of the Churches towards peace, justice and reconciliation within Northern Ireland. One thinks of the often unsung heroism of individuals, lay and clerical; the work of cross-community groups, often under Church aegis; the coming together of Church leaders, so tremendously valuable in symbolic and real terms; explicitly ecumenical ventures; the comfort given by the Churches in a context of violence and fear; the constant prayers for peace – and so on. The worship and witness of the Churches have contributed to the positive aspects of the Irish (and Ulster) character, for example the sense of individual responsibility before God for personal faith, moral living and the life of the community; and the capacity to absorb suffering through relating it to the suffering and death of Christ. The capacity of both communities in Northern Ireland for forgiveness is the fruit, often expressly, of Christian faith and experience. And we note finally that all the major Churches in Ireland are organised on an all-Ireland basis, so that Churches on the whole island, and not just in Northern Ireland, have a responsibility towards the difficult political situation.

However, it is questionable whether on balance one could evaluate the role of the Churches positively. Two recent reports, one by Duncan Morrow,[38] and the other by the Department of Social Issues of the Irish Inter-Church Meeting,[39] indicate why. In different ways they point to the reality that Christian ecclesial allegiance often serves to reinforce rather than to heal political division in Northern Ireland. Since this view is shared by many other analysts in this area (Wright, Hickey, Bruce, Boyd, O'Connell, Whyte, The Inter-Church Group on Faith and Politics), we present it in what follows as a view which warrants serious consideration by our Churches.

The nub of the case being made by Morrow and others is that for understandable historical reasons the Protestant/Roman Catholic distinction in Northern Ireland, allowing for exceptions on both sides, normally resolves itself into a Unionist/Nationalist separation. Religion reinforces political and cultural identity, which are themselves defined in opposition. Although this was not a religious war as such, still 'religious tradition remains the most consistent guide to political outlook' (Morrow, 3) and 'the most important badge of difference is religion' (ibid., 112).[40] This is not just a socialisation process, as if the Churches were simply reflecting what society would anyway teach its members. Rather, because the Churches can reach so deeply into personal and social reality, transcending all social institutions, they shape society as well as reflect it. And as long as the Churches remain so clearly associated with one particular political tradition, then through their influence on identity, values, friendships, education, important life occasions such as births, marriages and funerals, they tend to reinforce the divisions pertaining to these particular political traditions. Of course it would be simplistic analysis which suggested that the Churches are the only such reinforcers – economic inequality, for example, is a major cause of resentment and division. Further, Paul Arthur of the University of Ulster Politics Department has noted that in Ireland and especially in Northern Ireland there is a 'state of political pathology' which leads to an underdeveloped political culture in Ireland. Rigid adherence to the principles of the past and to the idea of compromise as betrayal has led to a failure of the will and ability to negotiate – dominate or be dominated! In addition, the effect of a 'culture of violence' has been to breed suspicion of any method of resolving differences other than by recourse to arms and violent methods.

But since religion is concerned with what is absolute and ultimate, religious reinforcement is particularly dangerous. It tends to encourage the notion of compromise as unethical. It has in addition the terrible power of uniting in hostility to the other referent group what might otherwise be a less cohesive community, with more treatable social and economic divisions. The result has been a diminution in the moral authority of the Churches; a diminution that is intensified by their impotence in the face of the awful violence inflicted on Northern Ireland and to a lesser extent, on England and the Republic of Ireland.

There are similarities and subtle differences in how this operates on the Protestant and Catholic 'sides'. In both cases religion is felt to give cohesion to 'our people', 'our side', so that Churches and congregations easily become refuges of calm in which I can be sure that none of the 'enemy' are present and in which I can experience a sense of at least implicit superiority. It is, of course, an oversimplification, but one can recognise a certain Protestant identification with the Chosen People and consciousness of the errors of Rome on the one hand, and, on the other, widespread Catholic identification since penal times with a theology of victimisation and consciousness of being the 'one true Church' with whom other Churches are in some kind of imperfect communion.

On the Protestant side there is the phenomenon of a political Protestantism which refers to the reality that very often religion is the thread which holds together different Unionist positions (for example, independent Northern Ireland/devolution/full integration within the UK) in their common opposition to the IRA and a United Ireland. Because of this 'political and theological Protestantism are now very often the same' (Morrow, 115) and the Protestant perspective 'provides a coherent political body willing to fight to defend Ulster' (Morrow, 113).[41] This is made all the more possible by a very deep rooted fear of the Roman Catholic Church, perceived to be the rallying force of Nationalism within

Northern Ireland and the power behind a confessional State in the Republic of Ireland. In this context a theology of separateness has developed, in which ecumenism is suspect. In addition, under the pressures of secularisation and of this political situation, the Protestant Churches have become prey to a congregationalism which shows a widespread fragmentation coloured very much by local conditions. It is difficult for Presbyterians, in particular, to speak with one voice.[42] It should be said of course that the phenomenon we are describing is by no means either entirely uniform or negative. There are, for example, considerable differences between the virtual fusion of the political and religious in 'For God and Ulster', particularly associated with Free Presbyterianism, as opposed to mainstream Presbyterianism, especially in more modern times. The emerging consensus between 'ecumenical' and 'evangelical' (as in Evangelical Contribution On Northern Ireland, ECONI) on the danger of idolatry and the need to forge a new common Christian identity is very welcome. Yet, while in Morrow's view the negative tendencies he has identified in his research are more prevalent in the Presbyterian than in the Church of Ireland or Methodist communities, he judges that in general the Protestant Churches are in a weak position to break out of this institutional identification with one political tradition.

On the Catholic side the position has different contours but the overall result is arguably very much the same. Once again religion and the Church are central to the culture and identity of the Nationalist community.[43] This is exacerbated on the Nationalist side by the difficulty this community has in identifying with the Northern Ireland State or constitutional reality, so that in many respects the Church becomes an alternative rallying point of allegiance. This is shown in situations where, for example, the Church speaks out about alleged abuses in security matters, when it is seen by Catholics as siding with the oppressed against official injustice but by Protestants as being a powerful anti-State force with a high public profile. There is of course a corresponding alienation on the Protestant side, especially among working-class people, who find it difficult to identify with any kind of present authority. This divided response is further evidenced within the Nationalist community itself, where within the ranks of Sinn Fein supporters the Church is very often viewed as a conservative agent bolstering the British presence in Northern Ireland, in particular because of its opposition to the IRA. However, precisely because of this quarrel with Sinn Fein and, indeed (as in the Republic of Ireland), because of waning influence among the deprived in general and among even middle-class Catholics due to factors such as Church teaching on sexuality (as the European Value Systems Study[44] has established), there is something parallel to the 'congregationalism' of the Protestant Churches operating within the Roman Catholic Church. Thus, although it can seem from the outside to be a monolith of great power and to have exhibited totalitarian mores within its leadership in the past, in reality its ability to impose the kind of change that would involve a less complete identification between Catholicism and Nationalism is more limited than that. Furthermore, while there is not any great fear of Protestantism within the Roman Catholic Church, there is a certain rigidity, for example as enshrined in legislation about Eucharistic sharing and inter-church marriages and in less than enthusiastic attitudes towards integrated education. Once again this religious justification of difference should not be underestimated: as the almost universal glue of the Nationalist community the Roman Catholic Church is in many ways stuck within a particular political tradition.

In the view of commentators such as Morrow, then, on balance it would seem that politics appear to dominate the Churches more than vice-versa.[45] To the extent that this is true, the Churches have become places of captivity rather than liberation with respect to the political situation. This can seem shocking, especially when it is clear that most churchgoers are ordinary decent people and that good relations at a personal level are the rule rather than the exception. However, as is often the case in divided societies, such 'good relations' are in fact polite relations which make day-to-day living possible at the expense of being able to tackle the difficult issues which keep people apart – 'Whatever you say say nothing'. An uneasy peace ensues, which covers over the deep fears which are avoided so that division is actually reinforced.[46] The Churches do not for the most part challenge this coded language of politeness that hides such deep fears – they have become not 'places of meeting with differences' but 'protective fortresses for threatened people rather than places of open and profound discussion'.[47] Furthermore, in so far as the Churches have failed to separate themselves and their faith from an identity with a political goal, they have, shockingly, become the organising principle and institutionalisers of the division between the communities in Northern Ireland.[48] It is in this context that the force of the phrase 'chaplains to the warring tribes' may be appreciated and the remark of Robin Boyd that because clergy see their role as limited to their own side it is often the case that 'the better they do their pastoral work, the more they reinforce the divisions in the community'.[49] This malaise is mirrored in the Republic of Ireland where there is a real reluctance in Church circles to consider what might be an appropriate Christian response in the Republic of Ireland to the Northern conflict.

As we said at the beginning, we believe that in many ways Christianity and the Churches have contributed in a very positive and indeed sometimes heroic way to a resolution of the difficult political situation on this island. Nonetheless we acknowledge that there is enough truth in the analysis of Morrow, Whyte and others to challenge us as Churches to review our overall impact on the political situation.

To exalt political ideologies to a status with semi-religious overtones and to bring Christ in as a supporter of these is a form of blasphemy and leads to sectarianism. This is so whether it be assimilating dying for Ireland in blood sacrifice to the sacrifice of Christ or whether it be that of making God's cause that of Ulster.[50]

Above all, in view of the ongoing attempt to make peace, we seek as Churches to offer a genuinely prophetic theological response at this time of uncertainty and yet of hope.

Our response

Very concretely, then, the Christian theology appropriate to the opposition of Nationalist and Unionist in Ireland will be a theology of reconciliation and solidarity. 'God… through Christ has reconciled us to God's self, and has entrusted us with the ministry of reconciliation… so that we are ambassadors of Christ, God making an appeal through us' (2 Cor 5, 18-20). God's reconciliation is once-for-all, but this 'indicative' challenges us to an 'imperative' of a ministry of reconciliation that does not happen at once.[51] Rather, it is a costly process involving some various attempts to come to a common understanding of the past, repentance of past wrongs, seeking to repair harm in so far as this is possible on the side of the offender, the exercise of forgiveness, the bearing of what cannot be put right on the side of the victim, and agreement by both parties to move forward in justice. As we said in our Introduction, justice is very much a part of this reconciliation. This is a justice which includes a role for conflict and anger as constructive catalysts of solidarity and intimacy, within a forgiving love. Such a loving attitude does not deny justice and opposition. It is in solidarity with the oppressed but in a way which invites the conversion of the oppressor.[52] In the context of Northern Ireland it is important to become aware that injustice occurs on both sides and, in particular, it is important to rescue the term justice from that semantic obfuscation which reduces it to social justice for one side only.

The term justice refers to the social imbalances which are found, albeit in different proportion, on both sides of the divide within Northern Ireland, but it refers as well to the greater issue which also affects both sides, namely the taking of life itself.[53] In this difficult process, which demands great patience and forbearance as well as realism and courage, the Christian is called to take the first step, to offer forgiveness in order to release that repentance and amendment in the other which are required for full reconciliation.

If we take this kind of theology seriously – and our situation seems to require that we do – then it would seem to follow very clearly that we need to be much more pro-active as Churches in our outreach beyond our own particular political and Christian tradition. In fact, just as the early narrative and preaching of the Good News received its focus and theological colouring from the particular crisis situation which the likes of Paul and the Evangelists found themselves addressing in different communities, so arguably our living of Christianity in Ireland ought to focus on this kind of reconciliation. Everything should centre around this, our Churches should mobilise their considerable forces with this end in view. It is in this context that the importance and intelligibility of the following basic principle becomes apparent: 'When there is tension over important religious values then Churches should opt for the interpretation which will enhance relationships in the interests of peace and reconciliation and ultimately of life itself'.[54] This principle does not ask us to compromise on truths which are central to our faith and which are securely held. Rather, it applies to situations where there are different views validly held within any of our Churches on controversial issues, asking us to opt for that view which best helps reconciliation, because reconciliation is important to Christ. This focus on reconciliation becomes all the more crucial at this time in Northern Ireland when the slow process towards the creation of a more normal political society needs all the help it can get.

Once religious identity is no longer confused with political identity, the way is clear to look upon compromise, not as a betrayal, but as a constructive achievement. While respecting the desire of most Catholics to identify with Irish Nationalism, and of most Protestants to see themselves as British, all citizens of Northern Ireland may still regard themselves as free to determine their own future, and to approve or disapprove of political structures which may be proposed (for example in the Anglo-Irish Agreement, the Downing Street Declaration and the Framework Document). To assert this principle, of course, begs the question of what kind of political entity Northern Ireland is. But this too must be subject to negotiation and compromise within the broader framework of relationships within Northern Ireland, between North and South, between the two islands and within Europe. The role of Churches is not to insist on one particular political solution to the exclusion of all others, still less to claim that any such solution is absolute or imperative on religious grounds, but to create the conditions in which political compromise becomes possible by giving an example of reconciliation based on forgiveness. Far from watering down Christian faith, this would vindicate it as a force for peace.

Questions
1. Can we identify ways in which the Churches have been liberating agents in the situation of political conflict in Ireland?
2. Can we identify ways in which the Churches have reinforced political division or have not helped to heal division?
3. What would be the practical implications of making the ministry of reconciliation and justice a priority on the agenda of the Churches?

II

THE CHURCHES AND A CARING SOCIETY

Ireland: Free State and Republic

The 1916 Proclamation had included the promise 'to pursue the happiness and prosperity of the whole nation and of all its parts, cherishing all the children of the nation equally'. This reference to the social responsibilities of the new Republic reflected the concerns of Connolly and Pearse, and the general recognition of the need to make the widest possible appeal. The coalition of literary men and Irish Republican Brotherhood members who planned the events of Easter Week, however, was preoccupied chiefly with the achievement of national freedom. In any event, the vacuum in political leadership resulting from the Rising was soon to be filled by the then socially conservative Sinn Fein. The Civil War was fought over issues other than the social direction of the new Irish State, though Michael Collins espoused a progressive social policy, insisting that national unity, economic concerns and social interests were all integrally related.

The Cosgrave administration of Cumann na nGaedheal was to steer the ship of State in a very different direction. Ernest Blythe's Finance Department pursued a stringent policy, cutting public expenditure from £42 million to £24 million in its first three years. The fiscal conservatism of Cosgrave was to be continued by De Valera, who adopted an isolationist approach which promoted self-sufficiency as an ideal for the Irish economy. As a consequence of these policies the first four decades of the Irish State were characterised by high unemployment and poor social provision, with emigration acting as a safety-valve. This socially conservative economic policy was, by and large, endorsed by the Roman Catholic hierarchy, which frequently issued dire warnings against the threat of atheistic socialism and communism. Whatever the precise role of the hierarchy in the

'Mother and Child Scheme', it can scarcely be denied that it was generally opposed to socially progressive legislation. The Protestant community in the South similarly did not see the need to offer a social critique of prevailing conditions. Its primary objective in relation to the State was to safeguard its interests in the spheres of education, medicine and other matters of direct concern.

Since the foundation of the State the performance of the Irish economy, and in particular its record on unemployment, has for long periods of time been distinctly lack-lustre. Apart from the economic expansion following the Lemass premiership and the re-emergence of growth in the nineties, the story has largely been one of economic mismanagement. Joseph Lee claimed that 'no other European country, east or west, north or south, for which remotely reliable evidence exists, has recorded so slow a rate of growth of national income in the twentieth century'.[55] This assessment of the Irish economy has been contested and is perhaps too negative, but it can scarcely be denied that serious errors were made and opportunities therefore missed. Moreover, having lagged behind European standards in the creation of a more adequate welfare infrastructure in the early post-war years, Ireland noticeably failed adequately to redistribute wealth or alleviate poverty. Although welfare provision did improve in the 1960s and 1970s, there is evidence that in *relative* terms, in recent years there has been 'a shift from the poor to those at the top of the economic scale'. Provision in health care, education and welfare support still remain poor by European standards, a point which is cited in the literature explaining the reasons for Ireland's recent high allocation of structural funds.[56]

Surprisingly, the current unprecedented level of unemployment has had no serious political repercussions. The political parties readily acknowledge the gravity of the situation, but they all operate within a broadly similar consensus, involving a conventional market-based economic policy. The oft-quoted comment of Jack Lynch that no government would be secure if unemployment breached the 100,000 barrier has proved to be untrue.

Fatalism and resignation no doubt have something to do with the apparent acceptance of 281,400 persons unemployed (seasonally adjusted figure, September 1996) – the equivalent of five million if replicated in a British context. Fintan O'Toole notes the degree to which Irish society has been 'shaped by famine and trauma', and how a deep-rooted fatalist mentality has in recent years been compounded by the New Right's scepticism about the power of the State to engender economic change. The Irish cultural determinants fit into a wider pattern. Western industrialised countries have of late shown a remarkable capacity for the relatively affluent majority to acquiesce with conditions of social deprivation which mean a sizeable proportion of society are, in economic terms, effectively excluded. In this regard John Kenneth Galbraith has warned of the dangers of what he calls 'the culture of contentment', whereby the economically successful ignore the needs of others.

The furore over the extension of Residential Property Tax shows how resistant the better-off are to reform of the tax system, however flawed the introduction of these particular measures may have been. A case can be made that the reintroduction of domestic rates would make it possible to take very large numbers of people out of the higher tax bracket levied on relatively low incomes and would provide incentive and reduce unemployment. Since property is an indication of wealth, as long as there is a rebate system for those on lower incomes, it should figure in any sensible and equitable system for raising tax revenue – a point which has been made by the Culliton Report and more recently by the Economic and Social Research Institute.

At the wider European level, Ireland's problems have been compounded by the fact that the European Union as constituted at present does not do enough to redress the centrifugal pressures of the market. Funds for economic development are too modest and the restrictions on intervention by the governments of member states are too severe. The consolidation of a single market in Europe is likely to place the countries on the periphery at an even greater disadvantage. Addressing this issue John Bradley and Eithne Murphy observe that 'in 1986 the Regional and Social Funds accounted for less than 15 per cent of the total EC budget and that budget accounted for less than 1 per cent of the total EC GDP. Hence, relative to the size of the EC, even a doubling of the Structural Funds between 1989 and 1993 does not represent a very large commitment of resources to deal with the problems of peripheral and less developed regions.'[57] There is a real danger of a two-tier Europe emerging, with a single currency for the more successful countries, if more is not done to counter the disadvantages imposed upon poorer member states by the current market-led ethos of the European Union. The advancement of alternative policies, however, is made particularly daunting by the inadequate democratic structures within the Community and by the autonomy of powerful financial institutions. The economic deficit is the product of a serious democratic deficit, which makes the real points of economic power inaccessible to popular influence.

The level of unemployment in the Republic of Ireland constitutes a human tragedy which poses a fundamental challenge to the Churches. In the past the Roman Catholic Church accepted in a rather conservative and uncritical way first the more isolationist economic policy of Ireland and then its shift to a more modernised, albeit inequitable, industrial economy. And yet the positive response to the episcopal pastoral *Work is the Key* (1992), the Western Bishops' renewal project, and other Church initiatives (including those of the CORI Justice desk) indicates an openness to more radical alternatives. This needs to be built upon if the Churches are to offer a social critique and a prophetic voice. Recent higher economic growth only strengthens the case for such a critique which calls for more concerted action by Government to tackle unemployment and increased social polarisation.

Northern Ireland

It is doubtful if the Troubles would have sustained themselves in the way they have done if sectarian conflict did not have some underlying economic foundation. Indeed, the salient economic factors which have provided such powerful sustenance to extremist Nationalist and Unionist ideologies can be readily identified. If we take unemployment, we find that it is not only disturbingly high in Northern Ireland, but is unevenly distributed between the two religious communities. Thus, in 1994 Catholic male unemployment stood at 22 per cent, over twice the level of Protestant male unemployment of 11 per cent. This kind of disparity is reflected in other areas of economic life, such as access to better-paid jobs. The efforts made to redress these imbalances by the Fair Employment Commission are to be welcomed, but inequalities still persist. Moreover, economic inequalities are compounded by the concentration of deprivation in specific localities. In the context of such inequality it is not surprising that the sense of grievance and injustice experienced by the Catholic community, and the economic insecurity felt by Protestants, have fuelled political conflict. Given the absence of constructive channels for democratic participation, there is a discernible process whereby the most threatened sections of both communities – the Catholic and Protestant ghettos – become fertile recruiting ground for paramilitary organisations.

Given that Northern Ireland is one of the most depressed regions of the United Kingdom, a case can be made that more concerted governmental action is needed to stimulate new investment, help redistribute wealth, provide greater equality of opportunity and, perhaps most important of all, address the problems of those areas with unacceptably high levels of unemployment. If such a policy were adopted the socio-economic basis of sectarian revolt would no longer be the potent factor it is at present. Cessations of paramilitary violence, appeals for mutual tolerance, political talks between different political parties in the North, or inter-governmental dialogue, are not enough on their own. Action needs to be taken to create the *economic* conditions which might facilitate a political solution. If this action is not taken there may be a risk of a descent into yet deeper violence, as disillusionment leads to despair. It needs to be realised that the search for peace must be related to questions of social justice, and is really concerned with the wider issue of whether or not our society is to be fundamentally transformed.

The costs of economic regeneration are quite feasible when seen in a British and European context. A combination of public sector investment and incentives for the private sector could make a substantial impression on the unemployment total of 86,200 (seasonally adjusted figure, September 1996). When it is pointed out that the population of Northern Ireland is 2.5 per cent of the total in the United Kingdom it becomes clear that the options are in fact wide open for precisely this kind of endeavour. To rely on the free market in a Northern Ireland context would be unwise. Such policies militate against depressed regions, since the market alone is unprepared to pay the cost of the social reconstruction required to achieve economic development. Political instability may be a disincentive to private investment, but there is no reason – apart from a lack of political will – why public funds should not be used to stimulate economic activity. This is already happening through capital transfers from the United Kingdom, but more substantial and better targeted funding is required. What is needed is not of course merely a question of throwing more money at the problem. An effective strategy would also require the provision of greater technical and managerial expertise, the brokering of international marketing agreements, policies to widen the skills base and measures to assist the long-term unemployed who at present are effectively excluded from participating in the market economy.

The Churches could help in the transformation of the economic situation by a more concerted attempt to promote a culture of solidarity in which the 'haves' of Northern Ireland society were more willing to make the sacrifices necessary to ensure justice for all. Despite some well-intentioned attempts in this direction, it is clear from the loss of allegiance to Churches in lower income areas that both Protestant and Roman Catholic 'have-nots' do not really believe that the Christian Church is on their side in this struggle for economic justice. While acknowledging the valuable economic assistance given to Northern Ireland by the EU and the US, in addition to the efforts of the Industrial Development Board, we see a particular role for the Churches working together to alleviate the effects of poverty and eradicate its causes.

With transformed economic circumstances and viable democratic structures, the religious divide would become less pronounced. A more open, and increasingly pluralist, society might then approach the question of wider political relationships and sovereignty with the pragmatism and good sense it deserves. Negotiations – accompanied by some movement towards the decommissioning of weapons – must continue to be pursued in order to formulate measures that would lead to greater political participation in Northern Ireland and a constitutional settlement that would preclude the domination of one religious community by another. These new arrangements will need to be guaranteed by a means in which each community would have confidence. Ways must be found to give ordinary people more confidence and a greater voice. A bill of rights, power-sharing and new forms of democratic participation are all needed. This would safeguard the constitutional rights of all citizens and prevent any return to majority rule, which becomes a travesty of democracy if the liberties and interests of individuals and minorities are not protected.

What is suggested is a generous and comprehensive approach to the search for peace which takes much more seriously the need to address the economic dimension in tandem with the securing of a genuinely democratic polity within Northern Ireland. All the alternatives to such an approach are unacceptable. Perpetuating the status quo of direct rule risks a return to violence; an independent Northern Ireland risks becoming a sectarian state; and lastly, the conditions do not exist in the foreseeable future for the creation of a United Ireland.

The Churches can assist in the creation of new democratic institutions and forums by accepting their historic responsibility to encourage the development of a more just and reconciled society throughout the whole island of Ireland. Fundamental to this process is the ability to define one's own identity positively rather than negatively, so that one no longer sees one's own tradition primarily as being in opposition to others. This would suggest that pluralism is an issue of considerable importance in bringing about reconciliation in Ireland.

Questions
1. How can the Churches encourage society to face up to the fundamental moral challenge of high unemployment?
2. What contribution should the Churches be making to the creation of new democratic structures?
3. How important is the economic dimension in the finding of peace in Northern Ireland?

III

THE CHURCHES AND PLURALISM

Introduction

Most contemporary societies are characterised by an increasing diversity of ethnic groups with their religious communities and cultures. This is sometimes described as a 'plurality' of cultures and beliefs. Over and above merely describing this new state of affairs, the term 'pluralism' implies a positive evaluation of it and suggests that it is possible to create a political framework within which this diversity can be contained. Whether knowingly or not, the general acceptance of pluralism, even by the Christian Churches, is based on the philosophy of liberalism which arose at the time of the Enlightenment in connection with the rejection of religion with its claims to universal truth and the relegation of pre-Enlightenment cultures to the 'primitive'. The strength of this philosophy lies in its insight into the mutual recognition of equality as the basis for social relations; its weakness is its tendency to restrict this to members of the propertied classes and European cultures, and its relegation of religion and associated questions concerning values and the ultimate truths about the whole human enterprise to the purely private sphere.

At the heart of liberalism is the demand that individuals – and, by implication, collectivities such as ethnic groups and nations – be given unrestricted scope for self-development. Their freedom in this respect is absolute, as long as it does not encroach on the freedom of others. This presupposes some larger framework in which the untrammelled exercise of freedom can be accommodated. The pluralist social order resulting from liberalism is built on the assumption that society can dispense with a basic consensus about values and meaning, for these too are subject to free choice. We thus need to distinguish between the liberal philosophy of the Enlightenment itself, the pluralist societies which have resulted from it, and the particular problems posed by pluralism for Christian Churches. Consideration of pluralism as at least a formal framework for the solution of Irish problems needs to be mindful of this background.

In envisaging the role of pluralism in such a solution it needs to be asked - with particular nuances for North and South – whether political pluralism can be justified independently of this liberal philosophy and whether pluralism, thus understood, is sufficient in itself to provide the basis for new structures. Is there a place here for conceptions of community which have their roots in eucharistic *koinonia* and ecclesial catholicity? The visible realisation of these in the Christian community could have unsuspected political consequences.[58]

In particular, the relationship between multi-culturalism and political pluralism needs further thought. Various political models are available (liberal pluralism, social republicanism, consensual communitarianism, regional federalism etc.), and these would need to be evaluated in the context of changing social and political structures throughout Europe. There is also need to re-evaluate the place of social solidarity and the 'common good' within pluralist frameworks.

Pluralism in religion

Pluralism confronts most religious traditions with a painful dilemma. For them, truth is an absolute value directly bound up with salvation. Their deepest instinct is to maintain their own continuity and stability, taking for granted that good order in society depends on this; the thought that alternative religious beliefs and ways might be just as valid as their own is inconceivable. Pluralism at this level of ultimate meaning seems to connote relativism, a problem which is now widely debated in theology and the humanities. The realisation that there may be other, socially viable, basic consensuses about meaning and values is perceived by some as a threat to the integrity of their beliefs, by others as an opportunity finally to break free of the constraints of 'universal' values. An additional source of discomfort to religious people is liberalism's insistence on the primacy of individual over community.

It must be asked, however, whose truth is in question and at what level. The *sect* insists on a version of truth internal to itself which consciously deviates from the prevailing norm in which it nevertheless participates (for example insisting on a special doctrine of believers' baptism by immersion in the context of the biblical and later traditions). The *denomination* shares with others a broad acceptance of plurality within a particular social and political framework. *Religions*, in the proper sense of completely disparate traditions, where they impinge on one another, differ more radically and may be unable to agree on the most basic principles. In Ireland *denominations* which in fact share considerable areas of agreement are in danger of behaving like sects because they imagine themselves to be different religions. It is for this reason that the *Churches* suffer the indignity of being labelled 'sectarian'. The captivity of the Churches in an inward-looking 'congregationalism' which is an embryonic form of sectarianism needs to be examined in this context. There is a linkage between the mutual respect which would enable Churches in different traditions to acknowledge one another's sincerity, and the political pluralism which finds room even for bitterly opposed interest groups and their viewpoints. An ecclesial practice of pluralism would not abstain from raising the question of the truth or value of others' beliefs, but it would define identity positively rather than negatively, that is seeing one's own tradition mainly in opposition to those of other Christians.

Liberal pluralism, as it developed in the tradition of the European Enlightenment, with its overtones of secularism, individualism and *laissez-faire* economic policies, is not necessarily the only available model of pluralism, whether in Church or in society. Alternative political structures may arise whose inspiration is drawn from other sources, such as the inclusive 'catholicity' of Christian *koinonia*. As the 'Vision' section of our document makes clear, there is much evidence for this in the New Testament. The doctrine of the Trinity, which arises from the Christian story itself, is a symbol of plurality. For Christians, God is conceived as the giving and receiving of love in what Paul Knitter calls 'the trinitarian paradox of both relatedness and yet genuine difference'.[59]

Implications of pluralism for the Republic of Ireland

The question of ethical pluralism, however, remains, and the Churches are divided by it as much as anyone else. This question is possibly even more important than the search for alternative political structures. It is not just the mere fact, but the quality of the pluralism realised in the Republic that will be crucial in introducing the subject into the Northern agenda in such a way that the recognition of two (and many more!) communities in Ireland is mutual and substantial, not just formal. Heated debates over ethical issues such as abortion and divorce have obscured the actual teaching practice of the Catholic hierarchy in Ireland, which has consistently been on two levels: addressing Catholics as members of the Church who are confronted with the practical options arising from such issues, and as citizens of a State which has opted for pluralism and must legislate for all citizens. Whereas in the former case appeal can be made to binding principles of morality based on faith, in the latter judgements must be based on experience and available evidence and are therefore open to disagreement. In such a framework there can be no such thing as a specifically 'Catholic' political or legislative programme, and the Church as such cannot give support to particular political parties and their policies, though the fact remains that the Catholic Church in particular, through its priests and activists, has given support to legislation which is in line with Catholic moral teaching.[60]

The Catholic Bishops, since the 1970s, have consistently indicated that in matters of legislation or of constitutional change, the issue to be discussed is not whether the teaching of the Church should be enshrined in law, but, rather, what is best for Irish society: 'What the legislators have to decide is whether a change in the law would, on balance, do more harm than good by damaging the character of the society for which they are responsible.'[61] It is vitally important to establish that this is the stated position of the Roman Catholic Church, not least because it is quite clear that a very substantial majority of Northern Protestants view the Republic of Ireland as a confessional state, so that the slogan 'Home rule is Rome rule' has more than historical credibility for them. But if this stated position is to have real credibility among Roman Catholics as well as Protestants, North and South, without thereby denying the legitimate interests and rights of the Roman Catholic Church to put forward its views on social issues, then we suggest that the Church itself could go further in stressing one particular aspect of its nuanced actual teaching. The Bishops would encourage a more healthy pluralism if they underlined the fact that there is a considerable difference between the teaching proposed to Roman Catholics in moral issues, and the advice that may be given by Catholics to the State about what to include in its legislation. The latter is not Church teaching as such, and the Bishops might helpfully say this more clearly, while hoping that their considered opinions on such issues be regarded as weighty by interested parties.[62] In doing so they would be making a very valuable contribution to a healthy pluralism, while maintaining their legitimate right to have views on the nature and development of Irish society.

Self-righteous 'tolerance' of inferiors or minorities is no basis for real reconciliation. Multi-culturalism is not mere variety; it must be worked at, by all concerned, on as equal a footing as possible. One area where this can be done is education, which provides a unique opportunity to demonstrate that pluralism demands more than mere tolerance, inviting us to enter into the history and the values of cultural and religious traditions that are different from our own. In this way they cease to be threatening and alienating.

Implications of pluralism for Northern Ireland

When the violence flared up in Northern Ireland the complex nature of the interplay between religion and politics was often not admitted, even when at least partly recognised. Well into the 1970s it was quite common to hear Church leaders assert that 'this is not a religious war'. In so far as this could be seen as a desire to avoid inflaming sectarian passions it was understandable, but at the same time was quite unproductive in terms of willingness to grapple with the deeper issues involved. Material of a serious and dispassionate nature was hard to come by. Such publications as *Holy War in Belfast* by Andrew Boyd (1970) or *Psalms and Slaughter: A Study in Bigotry* by Tony Gray (1972) were predominantly journalistic in style and aimed at the mass market.

Not unnaturally it was from the universities, where Irish secular history had been liberated from the political motivation of the previous generation, that much of the impetus for more perceptive analysis came. Another important stimulus has been provided by groups like the Corrymeela Community, whereby people of opposing religious and political traditions have found an opportunity to meet and face issues in a non-threatening environment. The Irish School of Ecumenics also plays a notable part.[63]

Now, twenty years and more into 'The Troubles', there is more general recognition and acceptance of the facts, both that Churches are to some extent prisoners of the troubled political situation and that they participate in its continuance in a variety of ways, consciously and unconsciously. Eric Gallagher and Stanley Worrall, in addition to various practical initiatives, made an important contribution in their book *Christians in Ulster, 1968-1980* (OUP, 1982), as the title of their final chapter indicates – 'Churches on Trial'.[64]

One must not overlook the marvellous work being done by many Christian groups of both main traditions, in seeking to overcome sectarian attitudes and to build a cohesive society based upon mutual toleration and respect. But the reality is far from the dream. In the political arena those seeking the support of the electorate have predominantly faced towards one section of the community or the other, with all too little attempt to see themselves as servants of more than 'their own', except on a one-to-one basis. While politicians inevitably have to rely upon a voting constituency for survival, it is disappointing to contemplate how far Churches have become imprisoned in the same mentality. In turn, the lack of strenuous challenge to this mentality by the Churches and of more determined effort to give witness to a gospel of reconciliation, makes it easy for each side's understanding and expression of the Christian message to be demonised and held captive by the other. In such an environment religion continues to reinforce political alienation and so the vicious spiral continues. How is it to be broken?

If what has been said to this point is accepted, it is obvious that political and religious initiatives have to work in tandem since their interests are so closely interwoven. The efforts to create a permanent cessation of violence on all sides are of crucial importance and it is right for Church voices to be raised in encouragement of politicians to 'get round the table'. But unless the Churches are themselves fully engaged around the table (or even the Table!), the one is almost bound to frustrate the other. Predominantly institutional models may have served the Church well enough in another age but by adhering to them now little long-term progress is likely to be made. This is a situation crying out for *koinonia*, not simply as a useful theological concept but as a lived experience of the Church. What does the complex word 'communion' mean? Fundamentally it is a matter of our communion with God and one another through Jesus Christ in his Holy Spirit. This communion exists through the word of God and the sacraments and manifests itself in the life of the Church as it engages with the world.

As many have noted, there is on both sides of the religious divide a very marked degree of theological conservatism and a puritanism largely out of fashion elsewhere. Regrettably the current revival of fundamentalism in many parts of the world is tending further to reinforce that element in Ireland, with clear implications for this whole sphere of concern. It is perhaps a major reason why ecumenical dialogue here, although quite well advanced in some respects, has yet to catch the imagination and take root at local level to any marked extent.

James Barr has noted the following characteristics of fundamentalism as it is commonly found in its Protestant expression (with both similarities and differences on the Catholic side). It is essentially a theology-less movement. Any Christian with his or her bible, believing the latter to be inerrant, can completely discount the arguments and opinions of any theologian who does not fully accept that principle. Since most theologians do not, this means that they have no function, indeed they pose a threat to be resisted at all costs. Barr maintains that, in so far as one can speak of a fundamentalist theology, it is fossilised, fragmented, resisting attempts to bring together religion and culture into any form of system, and inactive, since there is nothing for it to do except to restate or defend. Today the term fundamentalism is used, often without any clear or accurate definition, of individuals and groups who resist change in Roman Catholicism, Islam, Judaism and many other religious traditions.

While that may be somewhat sweeping (there are different degrees of fundamentalist thought) there is no doubting the fact that conservatism of this nature hinders the impact of those new ideas which might, without damage to basic faith, act as a solvent to rigid preconceptions of fellow Christians. Similarly, a puritanism which attaches great importance to certain aspects of conduct tends to exaggerate the significance of differences that exist. Neither is it conducive to tolerance nor concerned to look for a basis for reconciliation and common purpose. Indeed the concept of light and darkness, the elect and the damned, positively favours separation. Here again these characteristics are clearly recognisable as part of the make-up of some aspects of the Orange Order. Laying claim as it does to be primarily religious, while acting as both a political and a religious pressure group, it reinforces its own particular brand of conservatism, not without influence on local Church life.

The foregoing paragraphs might help to explain why such well-intentioned efforts as the Report of a working party appointed by the Irish Council of Churches and the Roman Catholic Joint Group on Social Questions, *Violence in Ireland* (1976), have had minimal impact over the years. Among other things, the Report recommended active Church support for peace and reconciliation movements and called for 'a sustained and far reaching programme of education within the Churches themselves by which their members might be made more aware of the political and social implications of Christianity for Irish society as well as of democratic methods available for promoting justice and peace'. In not a few places attempts to promote such a programme would require enormous courage and persistence, with the ability to withstand various combinations of apathy and outright hostility.

This is borne out in some of the comments recorded at the Churches' Central Committee for Community Work Conference in 1990, presumably attended in the main by less conservative Church members. In group discussion around questions on community needs, such as 'What can local churchgoers do?' and 'What initiatives do members of the group think they might take in their own areas?', considerable hesitation comes across in replies like, 'The Churches must be careful – when is it the time to come out as visible partners? Will the publicity generated be counter-productive?' The desire on the part of many for a new era in Church and community relationships is kept in check for fear of destabilising an institution that needs all its resources in the present situation.

Persons who have suffered a particular sense of grievance as a result of ecumenical hesitancy are those in inter-church marriages, whether in Northern Ireland or in the Republic, from whom many a heartfelt cry has come for help and understanding. While the Churches have repeatedly made a commitment to joint pastoral care of such families, that is to a practical form of Christian pluralism, the reality is all too often otherwise. Couples in such marriages speak to of their sense of 'falling into the gaps between the Churches', or say that rather than experiencing sympathetic pastoral care they discover the Churches to be 'a disruptive force' in their marriages. Lack of joint Eucharistic hospitality is a major complaint but is not the only pastoral difficulty and is not, of course, confined to Ireland. But added to the particular pressures of the situation here this highlights an opportunity for action that would be religiously and pastorally sensitive, a practical expression of pluralism combined with a firm Christian witness.

The pain of separation at the Lord's Supper and the urgency of healing that separation is eloquently expressed by Professor Norman Young of the Uniting Church in Australia: 'Seeing the Church as communion shifts our discussion of Eucharistic sharing into a different mode, in terms both of urgency and possibility... to persist in saying that sharing the Eucharist can occur only as the culmination of the process towards unity which God wills for his children is to persist in both a logical and theological error. No such intimate union can occur without our first being built up by sharing the Eucharist within the Body of Christ' (spoken at a meeting attended by a member of the Department of Theological Questions).

Finally, if the internal challenge facing the Churches is a formidable one, it is no less so when one looks beyond the immediate sphere of Church influence. Moving about the lower income sections of the community, particularly in urban areas where there is increasing alienation from the Church, one encounters another range of issues. Here, where the paramilitaries have had much of their base and where the vote for the more extreme nationalist and loyalist parties has often been strongest, Churches constantly come under criticism for their perceived irrelevancy. This is not, as might at first be assumed, for their unwillingness to espouse 'the cause', loyalist or nationalist, but for what is seen to be their failure to speak up for the most disadvantaged section of the community. One does not have to probe too deeply before being confronted with accusations of 'hypocrisy', the perception that for the most part Churches are content to let things rest, socially and politically, as long as their own members are not disturbed. While this may be an unjust generalisation, hearing it is a reminder that any hope of working towards a society whose members in all their diversity are equally cherished will have to take equal account of the social and religious dimensions.

IV

CONCLUDING SUMMARY OF THE ROLE OF THE CHURCHES IN IRELAND TODAY

We have noted some of the strong and weak points relating to the role of the Church in Irish society. What is required is a theology which comes from prophets (radical critique of Church and society), just as much as from priests (worship and life, sustaining the institutional life of the Church) and sages (care and guidance of the community, including pastoral work and the offering of insight).[65] This entails a clear rejection of any idolatrous identification between Christianity and political and/or cultural identity. It entails a clear call to enter into relationship with everyone – my neighbour now includes my enemy, and my group cannot simply be our Catholic and Protestant group but must include all and precisely that part of the all which is other than my natural referent group: 'Reconciliation in Christ frees us from anxiety about our identity. We exist in relation to him, not through comparison with those who differ from us.'[66] Of course, being human, it is proper that people more naturally identify with a particular culture or political tradition; but, being Christian, they ought to relativise the value of cultural and political identity in a way that opens them up to enrichment by what is other, even by what is opposed. The problem in Ireland is not so much that Catholicism and Nationalism, Protestantism and Unionism, for the most part reinforce one another. It is rather that the nature of the reinforcement in question is exclusivist, so that the other tradition is unjustly treated and there is little room left for political compromise. What is required is a different vision: in the end I know myself best through you who are different and other. A Trinitarian God is the paradigm of this kind of unity in diversity,[67] leading to a lived expression of *koinonia* within and between Churches. This is the God revealed

91

by Jesus Christ in his proclamation of the Kingdom with its subversion of established social orders in so far as they do not have regard to freedom and justice. This is the God who urges us towards a more economically and socially just ordering of society, and to a critically discerned pluralism. And this is a prophetic theology which operates within a biblically-based eschatological horizon which looks to the full coming of God's Kingdom at the end, but does not set limits to realised anticipations of it in the here and now.

Questions
1. If you have difficulties with Eucharistic sharing, are these primarily theological? How far may cultural and political factors be involved? What positive contribution could we make by a more visible unity between the Churches in Ireland?
2. What is the *practical* alternative to sectarianism in inter-Church relations?
3. Does Church teaching carry different authority when directed at Church members and at the *same* individuals as citizens of the State? Is there a 'public' and a 'private' morality?
4. Do you believe that inter-church marriages can help to bring about unity and peace?
5. How can the Churches take equal account of the social and religious dimensions of the conflict?

V

AN AGENDA FOR THE CHURCHES

The Sectarianism Report has highlighted a number of important issues that have to be faced, for example inter-church marriage, fear of the Roman Catholic Church, marches, the position of the Orange Order, flags in churches, Church and State in the Republic, Protestant formulations of teachings about the Roman Catholic Church, fair employment, equality of opportunity, and social disadvantage. The issue of marches has come into particular prominence as we finalise this document and needs to be dealt with as a matter of urgency. Further, a number of members are of the view that the Protestant Churches ought to focus on the relationship between their community and those Orange marches which are communally sensitive, particularly where there is a Church service involved. The possibility of increasing the opportunities for Eucharistic sharing, for example for inter-church marriage couples, is also something that needs to be examined. A number of members are of the view that the exceptional situation in Northern Ireland ought to encourage some flexibility in the rules on Eucharistic sharing. However, we wish to focus particularly on three specific proposals that the Churches may be able to take up as official bodies.

We are, of course, aware of the real limitations which all the Churches experience when they contemplate some prophetic action. Fired by the Gospel vision and by a 'politically correct' theological response, one might be tempted to propose some radical action that would simply not work and might do more harm than good. In the context of the tendency towards congregationalism and weakened Church authority in both Protestant and Catholic communities, the Churches are not in a strong position as institutions to be agents of change and blanket proposals will not automatically work.[68] We need then to be sensitive to 'where people are at' and to persuade towards Gospel truths rather than to impose them in a way that violates human integrity. And, as McCaughey points out, if the Church acts in a concerted way in the area of justice it may appear too dominant, whereas if it merely preaches it may not be effective.[69] Furthermore, as recent surveys have indicated (see especially the European Value Systems Study (1981 and repeated in 1990/1991), even in a strongly practising Christian society like Ireland there is a distancing of Church allegiance from ethics and the pragmatic 'ideology' or personal value system which guides Christians in everyday life. People are increasingly adopting a selective attitude to official teaching, especially in the sexual area. There is also evidence of some decline in religious observance, and a growing dissatisfaction with the Church among certain groups such as young people and women. It may well be then that in this changing religious environment the Churches are simply not strong enough to convey the kind of prophetic vision required. However, we should also note that the same surveys do indicate continuing high levels of support for the right of the Churches to speak out on issues of public interest – perhaps if the message were differently communicated, it would be received with greater confidence?

With such preliminary comment in mind it remains to suggest an agenda for the Churches which might contribute to a resolution of the crisis which has been identified.

Firstly, would it not be a positive step if all the Churches set up for themselves, in the manner most appropriate to their own character, a process whereby they would undertake a thorough review of their pastoral strategy, in the light of the reality of such terrible division on our island? This review or audit, a kind of pastoral assembly of representatives of all the People of God within a particular Church, should be with a view to turning around the respective ecclesical institutions in the direction of the reconciliation that is so urgently needed at different levels –

ecumenically, culturally, politically, socially, economically.[70] The focus on reconciliation is all the more important in the present situation. Of course assemblies on their own (see Vatican II and the Coleraine Assembly of the Presbyterian Church in Ireland) do not automatically effect change. Nonetheless, with clear terms of reference, careful preparation, a critically discerned process and, above all, a strong determination to make a concerted attempt to turn things around decisively, one might reasonably hope for substantial achievement.

Among the items one might anticipate as a fruit of this process would be a more impressive flowering of inter-community relationships, as Morrow urges – a mobilisation of Church resources in a systematic way to meet the crisis of our time. If politicians are being asked to do this, why not Church people also? Each Church would engage in this process separately, but there would also be a forum where results might be pooled and common policies formulated. This kind of review would have to involve every level of Church life, especially laity. It will not do that Church leaders say and do the right thing in this whole area – this is almost always the case anyway and is greatly to their credit. Rather, the whole point is that the institution needs to change and this cannot be accomplished by command from the top (even in the Roman Catholic Church). People have to want to change and thus be given the chance to 'own' this for themselves. Such a process would be risky – 'It may be that the Churches fear serious institutional division in the event of discussions on this subject becoming widespread'[71] – but with the paradigm of evangelical dying and rising as its inspiration, is this really a risk which the Churches can refuse to take if they wish to remain Churches of Jesus Christ?

Secondly, if they were to come together in a common confession of guilt, and a common desire for reconciliation in Ireland, North and South. This would be a bit like the 'Belfast Declaration' of 1986, but now between Churches, and not just

Christians. It would be more specific than that Declaration in naming our failures as Churches to be agents of reconciliation, along the lines of the Presbyterian Coleraine Declaration of 1992.[72] It could also be used in a liturgical setting, within local congregations and in inter-denominational services, perhaps with a period set aside specially with this kind of focus.

The thinking behind this proposal is that sometimes we start too far forward with ideas about reconciliation, neglecting to acknowledge our past and recent history of failure in this respect. It is only by allowing ourselves to remember and feel the pain of failure that we will really open ourselves to reconciliation recognised as God's gift, and not something that is entirely within our own competence to achieve. We need to do this not just as individuals, nor indeed only as groups, but precisely as institutions also. We need to do it also in the context of communal prayer, which has its own liberating dynamic. Could we also consider two other changes within a liturgical context, which could be beneficial and would not be too difficult to implement: prayer for other Churches in our official prayers of intercession: and, as with inter-church marriage, a common pastoral approach to the baptism of children of inter-church couples, which would include arrangements for participation in the liturgy of Baptism?

Thirdly, would it be possible for the Churches to take up the suggestion of 'ecumenical tithing', made over a decade ago by Fr Michael Hurley.[73] His aim was to bring ecumenism from the periphery to the centre of Church life by tithing our time, energy and money with other Christian Churches in areas such as formative reading, worship and social activities. This would be for those who wanted it, but facilitated by clergy and with back-up provided for the inevitable unsettling effect it might cause in the short term. Hurley noted that this was possible for Catholics in the area of worship if Eucharistic sharing is done without. Joining in the worship of another Church is particularly to be encouraged when it is a matter of the partners in an inter-church marriage worshipping together.

The Churches are challenged by the Gospel they proclaim to give generous leadership during this opportunity of peace. They are called to implement the basic principle about reconciliation identified by the Inter-Church Group on Faith and Politics by applying it to concrete issues that matter and that involve real concessions.[74] We believe that the agenda outlined above may help the Churches to respond to this challenge. Only thus will it be seen that we mean business. Only thus will we begin at Church level to answer the question which the Report on Sectarianism puts to each of us individually: 'What part of me is still keeping the conflict alive?'[75]

Questions
1. Would a systematic audit of the pastoral strategy of the Churches, with a view to giving priority to the ministry of justice and reconciliation, be helpful? Should this take the form of some kind of pastoral assembly or synod?
2. Should there be a public, ecclesial confession of sorrow and guilt with respect to the Churches' involvement in the Northern Ireland situation? Might this be an apt preparation for such an assembly?
3. What kind of dramatic or eloquent gestures might be made by the Churches which would make it clear to all, churchgoers and non-churchgoers, that we as Churches mean business in our approach to the conflict in Northern Ireland?

NOTES

1. Walter Kasper, 'Is God Obsolete?', *The Irish Theological Quarterly*, 55:2, 1989, p. 42 – a quotation from Kolawkowski. See John Paul II, *Centesimus Annus*, 24, 1991, where he says that the ultimate question of our existence is the mystery of God.

2. Martin Luther, *Weimar Ausgabe*, 30 1, p. 183ff.

3. *Catechism of the Catholic Church* (CCC), 295.

4. See John Paul II, *Veritatis Splendor*, 18, 1993, where he points out that God's law can be experienced as a burden if we live 'by the flesh', but that those who 'walk by the Spirit' see God's law as the way to practise love as something freely chosen and freely lived.

5. See *Salvation and Grace*, Department of Theological Questions, IICM, Dublin, Veritas Publications, 1993.

6. Max Mueller, *Sacramentum Mundi*, Vol. 2, 359.

7. John Paul II, *Tertio Millennio Adveniente*, 1994, p. 31ff.

8. *Presbyterian Principles and Political Witness Today in Northern Ireland*, Belfast, Presbyterian Church in Ireland, 1992, pp. 22-24.

9. Colm O'Grady, *The Church in Catholic Theology*, London, Geoffrey Chapman, 1968, pp. 242-244; Council of Trent Sessio VI, DS 1547. Cf. ARCIC II, *Salvation and the Church*, as an attempt to obtain some confessional agreement.

10. John Calvin, *Institutes*, III, 11, 1; III, 16, 1.

11. CCC, 1878.

12. Ibid.

13. Karl Barth, *The Humanity of God*, London, Collins, 1961, p. 77.

14. Cf. Rev. 5:10.

15. DS, 1501.

16. CCC, 83.

17. Vatican II, *Dei Verbum*, 8.
18. Ibid., 10.
19. CCC, 83.
20. Karl Barth, *Church Dogmatics*, 1/2, Edinburgh, T & T Clark, 1955, p. 597ff.
21. Jonathan Sacks, *The Persistence of Faith*, London, Weidenfeld and Nicolson, 1991, p. 61.
22. CCC, 2062.
23. John Paul II, *Veritatis Splendor*, 53.
24. Ibid., 96.
25. *Life in Christ, Morals, Communion and the Church*, An Agreed Statement by the Second Anglican-Roman Catholic International Commission, London, Church House Publishing/ Catholic Truth Society, 1994.
26. David Walsh, *After Ideology, Recovering the Spiritual Foundations of Freedom*, San Francisco, Harper, 1990, p. 267.
27. Ibid., p. 275
28. John Paul II, *Message for the World Day of Peace*, 1991.
29. Sacks, op. cit., pp. 63-64.
30. Ibid., p. 67.
31. Ibid., p. 65.
32. See *Peace, the Desperate Imperative*, The Sodepax Report to the World Council of Churches and the Pontifical Commission for Justice and Peace, 1970.
33. *Sacramentum Mundi*, 4, 381.
34. See, for instance, John Macquarrie, *The Concept of Peace*, London, SCM Press, 1973, p. 30: 'If we understand peace affirmatively as wholeness rather than negatively as the absence of war, then in some circumstances the gravest threat to peace might come not from those who were trying to stir up some kind of conflict but from those who supinely acquiesced in the existing state of affairs.'
35. *Pacem in Terris*, 35.
36. *The Church's Peace Vision*.

37. See Brian Lennon, *After the Ceasefires: Catholics and the Future of Northern Ireland*, Dublin, Columba Press, 1995, Introduction and Conclusion.

38. Duncan Morrow, *The Churches and Inter-Community Relationships*, Coleraine, University of Ulster, 1991.

39. Irish Inter-Church Meeting, *Sectarianism: A Discussion Document*, 1993.

40. Morrow, op cit., pp. 3, 112.

41. Morrow, op cit., pp. 115, 113.

42. Morrow, op. cit., pp. 114-115.

43. See, for example, James McEvoy, 'Theology and the Irish Future: Viewpoint of a Northern Catholic', in *Irish Challenges to Theology*, ed. Enda McDonagh, Dublin, Dominican Publications, 1986; Oliver O'Rafferty, 'The Catholic Church in the North of Ireland', *The Month*, December 1991, pp. 520-525.

44. *Values and Social Change in Ireland*, ed. Christopher T. Whelan, Dublin, Gill & Macmillan, 1994, chs. 2, 3 and 8; Andrew Greeley, 'Are the Irish Really Losing their Faith?', *Doctrine and Life* 44, 1994, pp. 132-142.

45. Morrow, op. cit., p. 122.

46. *Sectarianism: A Discussion Document,* op. cit., chs. 2 and 3.

47. Morrow, op. cit., p. 123; see also *Opsahl Report* 1993, leaflet ed. 15.

48. Morrow, op. cit., p. 119 *et passim.*

49. Robin Boyd, *Ireland*, World Council of Churches 1988, p. 51.

50. See John Thompson, 'The Churches in Northern Ireland - Problem or Solution?', *The Irish Theological Quarterly* 58, 1992, pp. 264-275, here p. 274.

51. See Duncan Forrester, 'Politics and Reconciliation', in ed. Michael Hurley, *Reconciliation in Reconciliation in Church and Society*, Dublin, Institute of Irish Studies, 1994, pp. 111-122.

52. See Gerry O'Hanlon, 'Reconciliation and Justice', in ed. Michael Hurley, op.cit.; *idem*, 'Solidarity', *Studies*, 328, 1993.

53. See Seamus Murphy, 'I don't support the IRA but...', *Studies* 327, 1993, pp. 276-286.

54. Inter-Church Group on Faith and Politics, *Breaking Down the Enmity*, 1993, p. 88.

55. Joseph Lee, *Ireland 1912-1985*, Cambridge, CUP, 1989, pp. 514-5.

56. Commission of the European Communities, *Community Support Framework 1994-99*, EU Commission, 1994.

57. John Bradley and Eithne Murphy, 'Ireland, 1992 and the Structural Funds: An Economic Perspective', *Studies* 311, 1989.

58. See John D'Arcy May, 'Political Ecumenism: Church Structures and the Political Process', *Studies* Vol 316, 1990, pp. 396-405.

59. Paul F. Knitter, 'A New Pentecost? A Pneumatological Theology of Religions', *Current Dialogue* 19, January 1991, p. 37.

60. See Patrick Riordan 'Does the Church Teach?', *Doctrine and Life* 37, 1987, pp. 19-27. Riordan refers to the distinction made by the Bishops themselves in 1973 between a 'private morality' and a 'public morality', regarding it as 'not totally satisfactory', p. 22, n.2.

61. Statement of Irish Bishops 25 November 1973, cf. statements of June 1976, April 1978, August 1983, oral submission to New Ireland Forum February 1984, and on many subsequent occasions.

62. See also *Presbyterian Principles and Political Witness in Northern Ireland*, op. cit., p. 11.

63. As evidenced, for example, by *Reconciling Memories*, ed. Alan D. Falconer, Dublin, Columba Press, 1988.

64. The Churches' own recent Discussion Document, *Sectarianism* is an honest attempt to face issues previously

avoided. Other publications include *Freedom from Fear: Churches Together in Northern Ireland,* ed. Simon Lee, The Churches' Central Committee for Community Work, 1990 and Duncan Morrow, *The Churches and Inter-Community Relationships,* op.cit.

65. See Terence McCaughey, *Memory and Redemption,* Dublin, Gill & Macmillan, 1993, and *Presbyterian Principles and Political Witness in Northern Ireland,* op. cit., *passim.*

66. *Sectarianism: A Discussion Document,* op. cit., p. 37.

67. See Gerry O'Hanlon, *Studies* 292, 1984.

68. Morrow, op. cit., pp. 116, 126.

69. Terence Mc Caughey, *Memory and Redemption,* op. cit., pp. 140-148.

70. See Gerry O'Hanlon, *Studies* 426, 1993; *Opsahl Report,* op. cit., p. 6.

71. Duncan Morrow, op. cit., p. 123.

72. See also John Paul II, *Tertio Millennio Adveniente,* 1994, 33-37.

73. See *Doctrine and Life,* 1983, pp. 410-414.

74. See *Breaking Down the Enmity,* op. cit., p. 88.

75. See *Sectarianism: A Discussion Document,* op. cit., chapter 10.

MEMBERS OF THE DEPARTMENT OF THEOLOGICAL QUESTIONS

Rev. Dermot Farrell

Rev. Dr Gordon Gray

Rev. Donald Ker

Rev. Feidhlimidh Magennis

Rev. Dr John Marsden

Dr John May

Rev. Professor Cecil McCullough

Rev. David Muir

Most Rev. Dr Donal Murray (Chairman)

Rev. Dr Tom Norris

Rev. Gerry O'Hanlon

Rev. David Steers

Rev. Ken Thompson

Very Rev. Professor John Thompson